Guerrilla!

By

Warren Littleton

This book is a work of fiction. Places, events, and situations in this story are purely fictional. Any resemblance to actual persons, living or dead, is coincidental.

ISBN: 1-4107-9416-4 (e-book)
ISBN: 1-4107-9415-6 (Paperback)

This book is printed on acid free paper.

1stBooks – rev. 09/12/03

CHAPTER I—THE PHILIPPINES

Lieutenant Loren Middleton had a spring in his step as he boarded his ship in San Diego harbor. He and the members of his Motor Torpedo Boat Squadron were on the brink of a great adventure. On that early fall day in 1940, they were on their way to the Philippine Islands. They would be one of the first MTB squadrons in that part of the world.

Dressed in his summer uniform, Loren saluted the quarterdeck as he came aboard. Tall and sandy haired, he looked the part of a Naval Officer. He saw that the ship was not very large and was crowded with naval personnel. The OOD told him that dependents were on board as well. He thought of Joyce. Perhaps she was right after all. This was no place for a family. He reported to his assigned quarters that he shared with three other officers. As the Exec of his squadron, he rated better accommodations than most of the others onboard, but it was still crowded.

The evening was pleasant as the ship pulled away from the dock and out into the roads. As he stood at the rail, he knew it was going to be a long, long trip to the Far East.

At chow time, he ran into Dave Blackmon. Dave was a JG and one of the other boat captains. Small and wiry, he was like a tightly wound spring, exuding energy. "Hello, Dave. Where did they stick you for this luxury cruise?"

1

"I'm up near the bow. I noticed that the whole bay moves up and down a lot."

"Have you seen any of the rest of the squadron?"

"Not so far. We're all supposed to be on board somewhere."

"By the way, our boats are going to be on their way as of tomorrow." In their last briefing, the CO told them that their six boats would cross the Pacific on the deck of a tanker.

The crossing was a surprisingly pleasant one, considering the number of seasick persons onboard. Loren learned that he had to keep an eye toward the ship's prow when he was on deck. If you saw someone running toward the rail, it was time to step back.

He and Dave ran across two of the other members of their squadron, Ensign Eskewicz and Ensign Kite, who saluted smartly when they came up. "Good to see you sir," said Eskewicz. "For awhile, we thought we were on the wrong ship."

Loren smiled. "We were about to come to the same conclusion. The rest must be aft of us. With the staggered chow hours, we may not see anyone till we get there."

They went on to talk about their new duty station. Tom Kite wanted to know about Cavite. "All I know is that it's big," said Loren. "It's located on the lower side of Manila Bay between Manila and the harbor mouth, according to what I have read. We are officially part of the Far Eastern Fleet. The other thing I know for sure is that the next few months are going to be a lot of hard work."

"Has anyone seen any of the dependents on board?" Dave wondered.

Eskewicz laughed. "Nary a one. I've heard a story though. One of them took a fancy to an ensign next door to me. She keeps sending him little samples of pubic hair in an envelope."

Amid the laughter, Dave shook his head. He was married, with a family in San Diego. "Now, I've heard everything."

Two weeks after they landed in Cavite, Loren and his CO, Bill Bainbridge, supervised the unloading of the boats from the tanker's deck. "Loren, work up a schedule for cleaning crews to get that protective goo off the metalwork and our machinist mates to get these engines running. I want these boats out on the water as soon as we can."

2

"Aye, aye, sir. Regular work schedule?"

"I want two shifts, seven days a week until we are running. In these times, we need to get ready in a hurry."

"Yes, sir!"

The huge, half moon shaped bay, enclosed on the west by the Bataan peninsula, was ideal for the running in that lay ahead of them. At the head of the bay was the island fortress of Corregidor and other smaller fortified islands to protect Manila from a seaborne attack.

Little time was available for extracurricular activities. Nevertheless, the crews found time to go up to Manila on liberty. They usually got back the next morning, slightly the worse for wear. Manila, known worldwide as the Pearl of the Orient, had many bars and cabarets with pretty young bar girls to make sailors forget that they were far away from home.

Loren noticed that Dave was becoming increasingly morose as they worked together on the boats. One Friday evening, Loren decided to talk to him about it. "I know you miss your wife and kids, Dave. You still need to get away from all of this sometime. Why don't you and I go up to Manila for dinner tonight?"

Dave's face looked strained. "I can't trust myself to go up there. If I have a few drinks, I'll probably grab the first girl I see and go to bed with her. Right now, it's really rough."

"I'll be the chaperone. I promise to get you back here if you look like you are backsliding."

"Thanks, Loren. I think you're right. I really need to get away."

They picked an excellent restaurant in Central Manila that specialized in beefsteaks. Both Dave and Loren were in civilian clothes. After martinis up front and an expensive wine with their steaks, Dave was in a mellow mood. He talked to Loren about his family. "Floradene wanted to keep our oldest in school in San Diego for the rest of the year. She and the kids will be coming out next summer. It's hard enough on dependents out here without having to have your kids adjust to a new school in the middle of the year."

"I know. I had a girl in San Diego. We talked about marriage, but she didn't want to come out here."

"I remember. I'm sorry it didn't work out for you, Loren. I wondered why you weren't running up to Manila with the others."

3

"No, I'm not heartbroken or anything. It's just that, after we broke up, I just wasn't interested."

Loren and Dave walked down the neon lighted street to the bus station. They both had much to drink, but Dave was feeling it more than Loren.

"Let's go into one of these bars, Loren."

"Are you sure you want to?"

"Yeah, I want to." His voice was slightly slurred. "I want to be able to say that I've been in one of these places anyway."

Loren and Dave found a booth in the back of the bar. The place was relatively quiet, with a jukebox and small dance floor. They had just sat down when two young Filipino girls walked over to them. "Would you mind if we sat with you?"

"Please," said Loren. He found himself across from a pretty young girl. "What is your name?"

"I am Eileen."

"I'm Loren. Nice to meet you."

A waitress came up and to take their drink order. The girls ordered a greenish, non-alcoholic drink that cost as much as the raw scotch that Dave and Loren were drinking. Eileen looked at him. "Are you an officer, Loren?"

"Yes, a lieutenant. In the Navy. Why do you ask?"

"I just wondered."

As they talked, Loren heard a soft thump. He turned to see Dave sprawled across the tabletop.

"Oh, boy. I've got to get him out of here, Eileen. Let's see if we can get him on his feet."

An hour later, Dave was sleeping peacefully in his bunk. With his head throbbing, Loren was not in much better shape. He took an Alka-Seltzer and settled in for the night. Morning would come early.

Soon Loren and the others were running the MTBs in Manila Bay and beyond, singly and in multiple formations. The engines, tuned to a fine pitch and tested in combat-like conditions, ran exceptionally well. The men worked well together, with a real sense of camaraderie. The long hours were starting to pay off. They finished working up the squadron in mid December.

Their CO, newly promoted, was away for staff meetings for most of November. When Loren and the crews demo'd the boats for him, Lt. Cdr. Bainbridge was effusive. "I'm really pleased with the effort put in on this, Loren."

"The men have really done a great job."

"Institute a liberal liberty policy over the holidays. They've earned it."

"Yes, sir."

Suddenly, they had little to do and Loren felt let down. The week before Christmas, he sought out Dave to see if he wanted to go into Manila again. When he got to Dave's quarters, Dave was lying in bed, with a flushed face.

"What's going on, Dave?"

"I've got some Oriental malady. Sick bay doesn't know how to treat it so I'm on seventy-two hours no duty. They gave me some APC and some of that cough syrup they call GI Gin."

"Well, you're in great shape. I don't suppose you'd be up to another trip into Manila."

"Not for awhile, Loren. Thanks anyway."

Loren found himself walking the streets of Manila by himself, with nothing better to do. He enjoyed watching the people, working in the streets. He had just passed a man who had a single desk on the sidewalk and an ancient typewriter in the middle of it. A flimsy roof of palm fronds protected him from the worst of the weather. A sign identified him as a Notary Public. A real optimist, he thought.

The time was late when he saw the bar that he and Dave had visited. He decided to go in. He was looking for a place to sit when he felt someone by his side. "Loren?" Eileen was looking up at him. "Hello, Eileen. I was looking for a place to sit."

"Come with me."

An hour later, the mood in the bar suddenly changed. The loud music became soft, dreamy ballads. Eileen and he had been talking about all sorts of things. It was nice to have a girl to talk to.

"Would you like to dance, Loren?"

The soft music hummed in his ears and he and Eileen danced on the crowded floor. He could feel her lithe body, pressed against

5

him. He looked into her soft brown eyes. She was so tiny, hardly any taller than his waist.

"Would you like to take me home tonight?"

He looked at her. "Yes, I would."

"See mamasan at the bar while I get my purse."

They walked through the darkened streets to her apartment. Naked in bed, she pressed against him. He took her in his arms. He had been without a long, long time.

The squadron moved into the New Year, proud and confident. They continued their simulated combat exercises, interspersed with occasional high-speed messenger duties and personnel transportation between Cavite, Manila and the "Rock", Corregidor. Senior naval officers who rode with them looked askance at the small, plywood craft, but the crews that manned them knew that they would make a difference if war came.

He saw Eileen from time to time as spring moved into the deadly heat of summer. It was on the weekends that he usually went to her. Early Sunday morning, he lay back on the soft pillow with Eileen sleeping by his side. After awhile, she opened her eyes. Then her arms were around his neck. She looked into his eyes. "You like me, Loren?"

"Yes, I do."

"Why don't we go steady? I will find a nice place for us. When you are not on duty, you can be with me."

He thought what to tell her. "Before I came over here, I had a love affair. It didn't work out. I don't want to be with anyone now."

"I'm sorry, Loren. Is there anything I can do?"

"Perhaps in time."

"Alright."

The balmy days passed, with no sense of urgency. They all read about the worsening relationship between the US and Japan, but it seemed far away and no reason for them to be concerned.

Then, Dave sought him out in his tiny cubicle. "Did you hear about the dependents order?"

"No. What's it all about?"

"The Navy says no more dependents here in the Philippines. I guess they're worried about this Japanese situation."

"I'm sorry, Dave. I know how much you were looking forward to having your family with you again."

"In a way, I'm glad. If things are going to get bad over here, they'll be safe stateside."

"That's something to consider."

"I wish I could be with them, though."

CHAPTER II—WAR!

Loren was sleeping in the early hours of December 8, when a guard wakened him and told him to report to the briefing room. Sleepily, he and his fellow officers gathered there. They were talking among themselves, wondering what the summons was all about, when Commander Bainbridge entered the hall.

"Attention!" someone called out.

"At ease, men." Commander Bainbridge stood on the stage at the front of the room. "At three o'clock this morning, we received a message that the Japanese have bombed Pearl Harbor." Suddenly, the room filled with a cacophony of questions and exclamations. "At ease, at ease! We have no further information at this time. Until we know differently, the command is going to a war footing as of now." He went on to delineate the many tasks they would need to perform. Everyone was in a state of shock. Wow, thought Loren, here we go.

The word passed was that the Japanese had landed large numbers of troops at Lingayan Gulf and were advancing toward Manila. Loren and his shipmates found themselves operating in a vacuum as the war raged to the north. The Navy, preoccupied with reacting to the onslaught, did not quite know what to do with them.

Commander Bainbridge talked to Loren about it as they surveyed their supply situation. "The MTBs are untried in combat and their capabilities are not well known in the command hierarchy. I've been trying to get us assigned to combat missions, but so far, no results."

"What do they want us to do?"

"Well, to start with, we've received emergency orders to relocate the MTBs to the Bataan side of Manila Bay at Marivelis Harbor. The Army is withdrawing to the Bataan peninsula, according to a prearranged plan, because of the invasion. They're supposed to hold until relieved. Anything that can move has been ordered to the peninsula, including us."

"What do we do when we get there?"

"We're to bring as much food as we can carry on board and go fully armed."

"That's unusual. I wonder what the supply situation is over on Bataan."

Loren supervised the loading of the 25 boat at the Cavite docks. They had four torpedoes in their tubes and every nook and cranny stuffed with food or .50 caliber ammunition. When they went to war, he thought, they would be ready. Their orders were for the MTB Squadron to anchor at a cove a few miles from the main base on Bataan.

Loren signaled his Exec, Ensign Eskewicz, to start their engines. Lean and athletic, Eskewicz looked at home on the bridge of the MTB. At that moment, huge columns of smoke appeared to the north of them, accompanied by the sound of many explosions. "I don't like the looks of that, sir," said Esky.

"Neither do I. I don't know why the Japs haven't bombed us down here."

"They'll be along, sir."

In minutes, they were out on Manila Bay, running at top speed. Clouds of ocean spray enveloped them as the three Packard engines ran at full power across the water. As the engines roared, Loren scanned the skies for enemy aircraft.

He talked to his Exec as they entered the estuary that led to their anchorage. "Bainbridge told me that, until about six months ago, there had been a native village here."

"Yeah, have a look. Some of the nipa huts are still there." Standing on stilts four or five feet above the ground, the huts were close around the gray navy buildings. Only a single pier was there for maintenance of the boats.

They had been there only a short time when Dave Blackmon came into Loren's makeshift office. "Loren, there's a submarine tender out in the cove. It looks like they're here to resupply us."

"Let's go have a look."

Moored at their single dock, the tender was crowded with sailors, busy unloading various items from her hold. Loren and Dave watched as they worked. Food and other necessities were available in abundance. "Maybe," Loren ventured, "the supply situation is not as bad as we originally thought."

"Let's hope. I understand they have torpedoes as well, but for now we're full up."

"I wonder if we can get some extras and store them somewhere. Let's go down and see."

The following day, the navy men watched as the tender left the cove. They were happy to get the extra torpedoes they had requested and looked forward to seeing the tender again. It never returned.

From under the protective umbrella of the surrounding trees, Loren watched the Japanese aircraft, in parade formation, fly toward their former base at Cavite. They had come for several days now, probably from Formosa, and no one was there to stop them. Loren had heard that the Japanese destroyed most of the American aircraft on the ground in the first few days of the war. Minutes later, he heard more explosions from across the water and huge columns of black smoke reached up to the sky once again.

Machinist's Mate First Class Jess Roe, standing at his side, looked on ruefully. "Well, Skipper, there goes our machine shop, spare engines and spare parts. We're not going to run very long without them."

"That's the truth, Jess."

In the days that followed, rumors abounded that the enemy had taken many of the islands of the southern archipelago. Another rumor making the rounds was that Zaboanga and Davao, on Mindanao, were also under enemy control. It looked to Loren like they were closing the ring.

Over the next few weeks, Bataan and Corregidor continued to hold. Loren's MTB squadron delivered urgent military dispatches from the commanders on Bataan to the rocky fortress just off the tip of the peninsula. Corregidor was a moonscape of shell and bomb craters and the majority of the buildings were in ruins. The military command, as well as the Philippine Government itself, crowded into the Malinta Tunnel and its laterals. A military hospital was in the largest network of laterals. In this incredibly constricted place, the Americans and the Filipinos stood against the Japanese onslaught.

In the black of night, Loren docked the 25 boat at the southern dock at Corregidor. He had dispatches for the Philippine Government from the peninsula. A waiting jeep whisked him across to the tunnel. As he handed over the dispatches at the government lateral, he saw a small well-dressed Filipino in a paroxysm of coughing. He suddenly realized that the man was President Quezon!

He turned to the soldier at the desk. "Quezon?"

"Yeah, that's him."

"He doesn't sound good."

"He's pretty sick."

"Doesn't MacArthur have an office down here as well?

"Right next to Quezon's"

"Is he here now?"

"No, not now. He's not here much. He prefers topside."

"They bomb up there all the time!"

"True. Somehow, he doesn't get hit."

"Hmmm. Well, see you next time."

"See you, Lieutenant."

On his way back to the boat, Loren heard the great guns of the fortress firing in support of the army on Bataan. Commander Bainbridge had told him that their sites, meant to repel seaborne invaders, were not very effective against targets on the peninsula. Although he made the trip several other times, this was the only time Loren ever saw any of the leaders.

Dave Blackmon was unhappy about their situation. "Jesus Christ, Loren, is this all they're going to let us do, be glorified messenger boys?"

"Bainbridge says that he's been bugging the Captain, but so far, no soap. They just don't know what to do with us."

"Pretty soon, the Japs are going to come in here and take over, and we won't have fired a shot!"

"I know how you feel, Dave. We're all itching to get a crack at the Japs."

Loren was sleeping soundly after a night run to the Rock when he felt a hand on his shoulder. "What?" he managed to say.

Dave continued to shake him awake. "Officer's call! The CO wants to see us."

"All right, I'm awake. Where and when?"

"Right now in his office."

Ten minutes later, the twelve officers were standing in front of Commander Bainbridge's desk. He rose and began talking to them. "As you know, things have not been going well for our side. The Navy is trying everything to slow down the Japs. Well, they finally got around to us. The Japs are pouring troops and supplies into Luzon up north at Lingayan Bay. It's our job to go up there and hit them with everything we have."

Loren found himself cheering and shaking hands with his fellow officers. "God damn, it's about time," someone shouted.

Bainbridge lifted his hand. "Listen up. The Captain says that there are no more torpedoes other than what we have here. The same is true for our fifty-caliber ammunition. Let's put 'em where they'll do the most good!"

Now that seek and destroy missions were finally forthcoming, the MTB squadron went after the Japanese with a vengeance. The enemy's shipping was at grave risk as the MTBs patrolled the bay and the shorelines of Luzon in the black of night. Their record was outstanding, with one of their boats credited with having sunk a cruiser. Loren's crew had so far sunk several supply barges and a large troop ship.

On a dark night, Loren's boat had a patrol up the West Coast of Luzon. Suddenly, the silhouette of a large ship loomed before them. Cutting sharply to port, they ran to the seaward as gunfire erupted from the deck of the ship.

Loren maneuvered the MTB so that they could attack the ship's port side as it moved toward the Luzon shore. They flashed through the water in the blackness, firing their torpedoes and strafing the decks of the Japanese ship. They left a trail of brilliantly lighted explosions as their torpedoes found their target, illuminating the sea around them like daylight. Grotesque shadows flickered across the boat deck as Loren spun the boat's wheel to point it toward the open sea. Being able to strike back was a great feeling!

Suddenly, machine gun fire rattled against the MTB's bridge. Ensign Eskewicz screamed in pain as the force of the burst hurled him bodily against the forward torpedo tubes. Loren, at the conn, could do nothing as Esky lay writhing on the deck. Gunner's Mate Ed Thomas saw what had happened and left his gun mount to go to Ensign Eskewicz, who was lying in a pool of blood.

"Get him down into the cabin!" Loren cried as he zigzagged away from the enemy fire.

The following day, they sought cover in an isolated cove overgrown by jungle greenery. Loren knew that they were vulnerable to air attack by the many Japanese planes flying over the peninsula. He and his crew watched as the Japanese aircraft crisscrossed the sky above their anchorage, looking for targets.

Thomas came up from the cabin and Loren turned to him. "How's Esky?"

"He's unconscious, sir."

"That's a blessing."

After dark, they made their way back to the cove and formed a stretcher party to carry Ensign Eskewicz to the field hospital, over five miles up the road.

Loren watched them as they went up the road. Then Gunner's Mate Thomas was at his side. "That's tough about Ensign Eskewicz, sir."

"He's hurt pretty bad, Thomas. It looks like he's not going to be able to return to duty."

In succeeding nights, they continued to patrol for targets. As long as their torpedoes and fuel held out, they would continue to fight. Their existence was moment to moment. The squadron's attrition rate had been high, with mechanical breakdowns and no new parts and supplies from their depots in the states. Somehow, Jess Roe and his counterparts kept the boats going.

In the past weeks, the Japanese destroyed two of their number in pitched battle. Laird's boat was able to pick up survivors, some of them badly burned. A number of others had oil in their lungs. With the current conditions, their chances for recovery were not good.

Until two days ago, the 25 boat was running well, but they had suddenly lost power on their way back from a mission. His chief mechanic had given him the bad news about the burned out main bearings in two of the three Packard engines just before morning formation. The squadron's chances were running out.

Now his crew, like the other crews whose boats were either disabled or sunk, was to report for duty at the front as infantrymen. The survivors of the other two boats had long since headed north.

Loren spoke with Thomas down on the quay. "Well, Ed, we did pretty well for awhile. Are you ready to be an infantryman?"

"As ready as I'll ever be. It's a shame we couldn't keep the boats going a little longer."

"Our seek and destroy missions against the Japanese are finished. We have some fuel left, but there are no more torpedoes and precious little .50 caliber ammunition."

"We have one good engine left on the 25 boat, sir."

"I don't think we could maintain headway with only one engine, Thomas."

CHAPTER III—THE NAVAL BATTALION

The deserted, navy gray Headquarters Building contrasted with the bright verdant foliage of the Philippine rain forest. Loren watched as acting quartermaster Ed Thomas issued arms and ammunition to the dozen men at the foot of the HQ Building stairway. He examined the Thompson submachine gun that the gunner's mate had just issued him. The scarred wooden stock and handgrip showed signs of hard use and he saw light places on the metal where the bluing had rubbed thin. An old weapon, he thought, old and worn out.

He looked ruefully at the small amount of ammunition that Thomas had doled out. "Is this the best you can do ammowise for the Thompsons?"

"I'm sorry sir. You and me have all there is."

The rest of his crew had Springfield .303s and bandoleers, except for one Browning Automatic Rifle. They had an ample supply of ammunition for the BAR, but not for the other weapons. Two other crewmembers besides Loren had .45 caliber sidearms and holsters. The acting quartermaster had issued six grenades to each of the men. Loren shook his head. Well, we're as ready as we're going to be to fight the Japs, he thought.

He called the men to attention. "When you have drawn your weapons, clean them and arrange your packs for the trek north tomorrow morning. We'll head out at 0800. Thomas, issue some rations for the trip as well."

"Aye, Aye, sir." His portly, red haired, acting quartermaster headed for the storage shed.

Their final orders as a PT Boat Squadron had come down, with all operational boats ordered to Corregidor. Since they had no cover at all there in daylight hours, Loren assumed that this was just a temporary destination and they would be shoving off again quickly. His boat, number 25, was still at the quayside.

Their commanding officer, Lieutenant Commander Bainbridge, trim in his tropical wools, had addressed them before the three remaining operational boats headed out for Corregidor the previous night. "I want to thank all of you for volunteering to be part of the Naval Battalion. As you know, the battalion is forming up near the front lines on the Bataan peninsula. I'm sure you will all carry on in the naval fighting tradition up there with the army."

Loren had listened in silence as the commander spoke. In fact, they had had little choice in the matter of volunteering. The battalion had sent a Marine Corporal to escort them back to the battalion base camp. If other options existed, Loren was unaware of them.

As he watched each man draw his arms, Loren had no illusions about their situation. Tomorrow, they would be going up to the front lines in what would ultimately be a losing battle, a battle that for them could end only two ways, death or imprisonment. From the word that had spread about their treatment of POWs, Loren had made a conscious decision not to become a prisoner of the Japanese. They had little ammunition and few medical supplies. Until his time ran out, he would kill as many Japs as he could.

Loren arranged the equipment issued to him on the top of his footlocker and then looked around. He would probably not sleep under a roof again for a long time. He planned to hike over to the field hospital to see Ensign Eskewicz one last time before they left. Because of the seriousness of his condition, he and a handful of others remained in the field hospital when they evacuated the rest of the wounded to Corregidor. Two of the nurses volunteered to stay behind with them.

Loren called his crew together after lunch. "I'm going to hike over to the field hospital to see Esky one more time before we leave. Any of you who would like to come along are welcome." He saw some knowing smiles among the men. His crew knew about JoAnne.

He had met her when he had first gone to visit his exec after the mission. JoAnne was in charge of Esky's treatment, which she performed with competence and caring. He had seen this side of her during his visits and liked her because of it.

She was of medium height, slender with chestnut brown hair and lovely brown eyes. Her complexion was deeply rosy, almost ruddy. She was an attractive woman, even in the olive drab coveralls that the nurses wore. JoAnne told him that they wore starched white uniforms when they had first come to the Philippines, until the Japanese destroyed their laundry. When they first talked together, she was warm and friendly and he wished they had time to get to know each other.

All of his crew had chosen to go along and, after an hour and a half or so, they arrived at the hospital. JoAnne saw them coming and went to him.

"How's he doing, JoAnne?" She seemed to him to be especially pretty that day.

"Maybe a little better. It's a godsend that we have some sulfa so that we can control any kind of infection."

They walked toward the building where the remaining patients were. The field hospital was a series of Quonset Huts set in a clearing in the middle of the jungle. Large tents, set up for overflow when the main buildings were full, surrounded the huts. The Army had painted a red cross on a white field on the roof of the largest building.

They went into the hut where Esky was. The other wounded, some of them completely swathed in bandages, lay still on their beds. Medicinal smells permeated the air. Esky was awake and smiling.

"You ready for that foot race now?" asked Loren. His exec had been a 440 champion at Annapolis.

"Give me a little more time and I'll whip your ass."

"I believe it." Esky looked gaunt and feverish to Loren as they talked together. Loren told him about their orders and their destination.

"Then this is it, huh?"

"For the time being, Esky. Who knows where we'll all be, even next week."

In a half-hour, JoAnne came to tell them that her patient needed to rest. He was noticeably less responsive than when they had first arrived.

"Hang in there, guys."

"You do the same, Esky."

JoAnne came to his side as he left the tent. "I won't be seeing you any more, then."

"It doesn't look that way."

"It's been nice knowing you, Loren."

"I've enjoyed knowing you as well."

He said hello to Beverly Jones, the other nurse who stayed behind, as JoAnne and he walked toward the road. Bev was quiet and withdrawn. The rest of his crew were waiting and they set out down the rough road. JoAnne stopped a short distance from them and watched the men move away. As he looked back at her, she waved.

Trudging down the long road to the cove, he thought about JoAnne. He wondered what would happen to her and to Bev, now that the struggle was almost over. JoAnne was very nice and, in a normal world, they might have developed a relationship, but there was no question of that now. As he continued down the road, he reflected on how little control they had over their lives.

Loren entered the barracks and lay down on his bunk. He stared at the ceiling and wondered again what tomorrow would bring. Everyone else around him was apparently asleep. He had been there for perhaps a half-hour when he heard the deep, throbbing sound of an MTB coming slowly up the inlet.

Loren threw on his shorts and a shirt and ran for the water. The others had heard as well and were running in the same direction. Through the gloom, he could make out a boat moving very slowly and low in the water, with bow waves lapping at the gunwales. After several minutes, he was able to make out the number on the hull. The boat was Lieutenant Blackmon's and it looked in danger of foundering.

The boat came on steadily and finally ran aground lightly on the sandy beach of the cove. Water was pouring from a large hole below the waterline. A small, wiry figure vaulted over the side and waded the last few feet to shore. Loren recognized Dave Blackmon in the gloom. His crew was following close behind.

Loren went to him and the two men shook hands. "Hello Dave. I didn't think I'd be seeing you again, at least not this soon. What happened to your boat?"

Dave was downcast. "We hit a reef in some shallow water when we were out about an hour from shore. We've been trying to effect repairs up in an inlet all day. The patch we came up with seemed to be working when we were stationary, but it started to leak as soon as we got under way. We bailed out as much water as we could and started for here. We were hoping that you guys could help us to get the hull patched up."

"We'll have to wait till morning to get a look at how bad it is. You're lucky that you caught us. Those of us that are left were planning to march up to the front lines and join the Naval Battalion tomorrow."

"My crew needs some rest. Let's get together and look at our options in the morning."

"Roger." They headed back to the barracks.

Dave and Loren examined the gaping hole in the 28 boat's hull at first light. Loren used a tape measure to check the extent of the damage. "I can't see that we have anything that could be used to shore up that hole."

"It doesn't look good, does it."

"The Naval Battalion can always use a few more men." Lt. Blackmon said nothing.

CHAPTER IV—DELIVERANCE!

Jess Roe sought out Loren later that morning. Jess was the Machinist's Mate First Class in charge of maintenance on the 25 boat. Whether he was hard at work or relaxing, Jess always looked like he was in a sweat from excessive activity. The thick glasses that he wore accentuated his earnest expression.

"Skipper, I went down to have a look at Lieutenant Blackmon's boat. You know, we have some options that we didn't have before now."

"What do you have in mind, Jess?"

"We can cannibalize the main bearings from the 28 boat's engines and, with a bit of luck, get the 25 boat running again."

"I thought about that earlier and wondered if it was doable. The prospect's exciting! How long do you think it would take to get it up and running?"

"Those engines have got some water in them now and that's going to make things more difficult. I think that with Scott, the 28 boat's maintenance guy, to help, we could probably put things together in a couple of long days. You know him, Skipper, he's the roly-poly guy with gray hair."

"Yes. That's got a tremendous appeal, Jess. We have a lot of other things to decide if we do get the 25 boat up and running, like where do we go with it. I'll chart out some possibilities and we'll have a general meeting with everyone at one o'clock. This course could be hazardous and we'd have to undertake it on a volunteer basis only. Some of our people might prefer the Naval Battalion. At least that situation is predictable. You and Scott get started on what needs to be done and I'll see you and the others at one o'clock in the mess hall." He spent the rest of the morning discussing options with Dave.

Dave was excited when Loren told him about Jess' proposal. "That sounds great! I was thinking about how far we might get with the one engine that's working. If we can get all three up and running, we can go just about anywhere our remaining fuel would take us."

"It sounded good to me, too. Let's have a look at the charts and see where we might head for."

At one, Loren explained Jess' proposal and the risks entailed to the combined crews. "If we are fortunate enough to get the 25 boat operational again, there's no guarantee that we won't break down out on the open sea and be sitting ducks for the Jap navy. Lt. Blackmon and I have discussed possible destinations and the best one seems to be Mindanao. When we last heard, we still have some kind of military presence there. Our fuel supply will be critical. We don't have a lot and someone added paraffin to some of it. It's out and out sabotage. We'll have to strain it before we can leave.

"What happens after we go ashore is hard to say at this time. Our chances certainly would be a lot better than if we stay here on the Bataan peninsula. I'm going to ask for volunteers. If anyone chooses not to go, there's the Naval Battalion. Let's have a show of hands as to who wants to go."

Without hesitation, the two crews volunteered to a man. Even the Marine, Corporal Buchman, sent to show them the way to the Naval Battalion, had voted to go. Tall and muscular, with close-cropped red hair and pale blue eyes, he was the consummate warrior. Loren was happy that he would be with them for whatever lay ahead.

"I'm glad that we're all going to be in this together, even though it's going to be a bit cozy on the 25 boat. Jess and Scott have already started on the bearings. We are all here to help you, Jess, so sing out if you need us."

As they were dispersing, Loren heard the sound of an aircraft engine. "Everyone take cover!" he shouted as he headed for the nearest revetment, his pulse pounding. The single engine seaplane passed low over their base, the Japanese insignia prominently displayed. The plane then droned off into the distance. Loren clambered out of the revetment and motioned everyone to gather around. "Keep a sharp lookout, now! The Japs will probably be back very soon, especially with the 28 boat sitting out there. Stay on your toes!"

In less than an hour after the seaplane appeared, they heard the sound of multiple engines heading their way. In seconds, three Nakijima 97 dive bombers passed low over them. They climbed rapidly and circled back, getting ready for a bombing run. Loren peered over the edge of their dugout and saw the bombs falling as the Nakijimas dived toward them. Tremendous explosions erupted out in the water followed by more explosions almost on top of them. The HQ building's roof shattered and the interior burst into flame. Dirt, splinters of wood and large chunks of plaster rained down on the people in the revetment.

One of the bombs fell close to the revetment across the way. "Someone's been hurt over there!" cried Dave.

As the engine noise receded, Loren, Dave and the others left the shelter and ran to the other side. Buchman raised his head as they arrived. "One of the torpedomen from Lieutenant Blackmon's crew took some shrapnel in the throat. He's dead."

Everyone else seemed to be all right, though some of them couldn't hear for the moment. They looked out into the cove, but, miraculously, neither of the boats looked damaged, despite some near misses.

Loren was the first to notice the column of smoke coming from the direction of the field hospital. As they stared, a jeep came careening down the road and entered the base.

JoAnne leapt from the driver's seat and ran towards them. She appeared badly shaken. "There were at least two direct hits on the hospital! There is nothing but smoke and flame! Please come and help!"

Loren and three others jumped into the jeep and headed back up the bumpy, rutted dirt road to the site. Ed Thomas was driving while Loren held JoAnne who was trembling like a child. By the time they arrived, the fires had pretty much burned themselves out. The explosions had leveled most of the buildings, except for two towards the rear of the compound that the bombs missed. The four men and JoAnne searched desperately for signs of life.

Loren determined immediately that Esky was dead. The charred remains were not pretty to see. The others searched through the bombed out ruins of the buildings. Two of the blackened corpses were still in their shattered hospital beds. Only parts of the others were visible. Loren took several deep breaths to get hold of his emotions.

Then JoAnne called him. "I've found Bev. She's still alive." He rushed to her side. Half buried in rubble, Bev's eyes stared uncomprehendingly at them. "She's in shock. It looks like she has a concussion as well. Help me get her up."

With some effort, Loren removed the tangle of wooden beams and the large sheet of corrugated metal that had her pinned to the ground. He helped JoAnne lift her cautiously to her feet. She appeared to be unhurt, except for a cut in her hairline.

"We've got to get them out!" Bev screamed and then lapsed again into silence.

Loren looked at her closely. "Let's get her back down to the cove where she can rest and be quiet." He looked around him at the destruction. "What's in those two buildings?"

"Mostly medical supplies. There's some basic foodstuffs as well."

"We need to come back here and go through them to see what we might be able to utilize for our projected cruise."

"Cruise?" asked JoAnne.

"A lot has happened since I saw you yesterday. We may be able to get the 25 boat running again. I'll tell you about it when we get back to the cove."

The jeep ran out of fuel on the way back and Loren carried Bev in his arms the rest of the way to the base. She appeared to be in a deep sleep and was not aware of what was happening around her.

Jess, Scott, and the two helpers they had commandeered were working around the clock to rebuild the 25 boat's engines. Loren came down to see how they were doing and Jess came over to report. "Sir, the engines are not in good condition. They have double the hours of service on them without overhaul and tuning. We'll have to reuse the old gaskets, because there are no new ones, and there is no sealing compound either."

"You'd better take special care with those gaskets. If they fall apart on you, we won't be going anywhere."

"We'll treat 'em like they was gold, sir."

They both knew that the 25 boat's bottom needed scraping and the struts needed an overhaul, but no time remained to do it. One of the repair crew would catnap while the others continued. The threat of Jap aircraft pushed them on because, if they returned, all their work would be for naught. The repair team worked in the dark of night with only a shaded bulb to help them see. Lights seen from the air would also be fatal.

The next morning, Loren organized a party to hike back to the hospital and bring back anything they found that could be of use. He found JoAnne in the barracks. "Would you come along and help us select the most important medical supplies from the stores up at the hospital?"

She smiled as she replied. "Of course. Give me a few minutes to get ready."

Her enthusiasm was catching. Since he had told her of their plan to escape the peninsula, she had a new spring in her step. Loren had noticed it in the others as well. They hiked up the trail to the hospital that morning. When they reached the site, they set about their task. Loren organized a grave detail to bury the dead and, when they finished, he recited what he could remember of the naval burial service.

Loren spoke to Dave afterwards. "Did Bainbridge give you any information on where the Japs are now? We've lost touch these last few days."

"No, he didn't. The only thing I know for sure is that the artillery barrages are a lot nearer than they were."

"Yeah, I know. To be safe, I'm going to set out a picket line for the working party. The Japs may be closer than we think."

He was standing a few yards from the nearest man with his Thompson cradled in his arm when he saw a movement by the furthest building. He brought the Tommy gun to the ready and sent a waist high burst spattering against the building wall. A man immediately showed himself with his hands raised high. He was a Filipino, in a navy uniform!

Loren motioned him to come closer and the man responded. "Yes, sir, I am coming!" When he stood in front of him, Loren saw that he wore the insignia of a Steward's Mate. He was a portly man with a large black mustache.

"Who are you?" Loren asked.

The man answered in a heavily accented voice. "I am Ramon Vargas, the Chief Steward's Mate for the hospital. I was away foraging when the bombing started."

By that time, members of the two crews had surrounded him. His naval ID was in order and Loren wound up welcoming him to their midst. Dave Blackmon was clearly unhappy and pulled Loren aside. "What do we want with this Filipino? He's just one more mouth to feed."

"Have you seen all of the flour, powdered eggs, and things in their larder? How good are you in combining them into something edible?" Dave said no more. Loren briefly explained to the Filipino what they were planning and asked if he would like to join them.

"I would like to go with you very much. I can be useful to you because I know the islands well."

His first duty with his new command was to help transport the food they had liberated from his larder to the base. The trip back was much more difficult, with each man toting a heavy load. JoAnne carried what she could as well. The canvas straps that supported Loren's load cut painfully into his chest and shoulders. He and the others pressed on toward their base. They had no time to stop and rest. After a long, arduous march, they arrived at the cove. Everyone who was not on guard duty or working on the engines slept soundly that night.

Early the next morning, Loren awakened to the sound of one of the big Packard engines turning over and catching. The other two followed close behind. He slipped into his uniform and walked down to the quayside.

A very tired group of mechanics greeted him. Jess was beaming. "I think we got 'em running, Skipper!"

"Terrific! Do you think you can move the boat over close to the bank and anchor there? We can cut some palm fronds and the Japs won't even know we are here."

"Do it right away, Skipper." An hour later, the repair crew was sleeping heavily and Loren was organizing the final tasks to get them on their way, mainly the loading of provisions and equipment. The crew gathered around him as they discussed what they had left to do.

Dave spoke up. "If we are going any distance, we are going to have to carry some extra fuel on deck. All we have are fifty gallon drums."

Jess Roe shook his head. "That's going to be a lot of extra weight. That deck is only 3/8 inch plywood."

"We should be able to reenforce it somehow," Loren interjected. "Jess, take a look at the navy buildings and see if we can find some planking to reenforce the decks."

"Aye, aye, Skipper."

"Dave, see what kind of an arrangement you can manage for carrying drums of fuel on deck. We'll need as much as we can carry."

"Roger."

They were able to reinforce the deck with planking taken from one of the undamaged buildings. After much discussion, they agreed they could carry twenty fifty-gallon drums on deck, a total of an additional 1000 gallons. The 25 boat had an internal fuel capacity of 2000 gallons of the highly volatile, hundred-octane airplane grade gasoline.

Dave looked ruefully at the lashed down drums on the deck of the 25 boat. "When we've consumed all this fuel, we had better be at our proposed destination."

"By definition," Loren replied.

The fifty caliber magazines on the boat were full and additional cartridges stored below decks. As the others worked through the day, three of the crewmen patiently strained the sabotaged fuel through a chamois.

Loren held a final briefing. "The Japanese were getting quite close now and, as best as we can judge, the U.S. infantry has retreated to their last line of defense on the peninsula. Our scheduled departure time is at 2100 hours this evening. Everyone try to get a little rest. It's going to be a long night." They had been lucky so far, he thought. The skies were clear of Japanese aircraft.

When he went to see JoAnne, he found that Bev had recovered somewhat and was helping to sort out the medical supplies. He spoke to her as she was sorting bandages. "How is it going, Bev? Are you feeling better, now?"

"I'm OK."

There was a long silence. He looked at JoAnne, but she only shook her head, imperceptibly.

"All right. Be ready to go at 2100." As he walked back to the boat, he was concerned about her. He hoped that time would make things better.

Loren watched the crews load fuel and supplies aboard the 25 boat, as preparations continued for their departure. For the first time in a long while, he thought about how it had all begun for him, growing up in Baltimore, Maryland and his time at the Naval Academy.

CHAPTER V—THE NAVY

Loren graduated from Annapolis, Class of '34, and began his career in the peacetime U.S. Navy. It seemed to him as if it were only yesterday. He had been born and raised in Baltimore, practically in the shadow of the Naval Academy. He was tall, with sandy hair and blue eyes, and those who knew him considered him personable and intelligent.

He remembered the trauma his family felt, in the midst of the Depression, when they could not raise the money for his college education. Looking for ways to achieve his goal, he had at last taken the entrance exam to qualify for the Naval Academy.

He had done well in school and placed high on the test. His personal interviews had gone well and he seemed to be what the Navy was looking for in an officer. The interviewing officer had given him a beneficent smile at the conclusion of his processing. His appointment had followed shortly after.

His four years at the academy had gone by quickly and he had graduated in the top ten percent of his class. His high school sweetheart, Kristen, had been there for him during these years. He thought of her and their first fumbling attempts at passion after the Ring Dance during his second year.

The environment at Annapolis was not conducive to developing meaningful relationships with members of the opposite sex. When he had graduated and was able to lead a more or less

28

normal life as a Naval Officer, he found that he hardly knew Kristen. She had wanted to marry immediately, but he felt that they needed more time together before they took so serious a step.

He remembered the hurt look in her eyes when he talked to her. "You don't want to marry me?"

"Kris, this is only the third or fourth time we have been alone together since high school. Give it some time."

"I've given you everything, Loren."

"I know."

"Either you want to marry me or you don't."

Loren remembered the dire feelings that he had. "I just think we need more time." After that, they drifted apart.

His first duty station was at Pearl Harbor in the Hawaiian Islands on a destroyer. Excited by the prospect, he enjoyed the long train trip across the country to San Diego and his new ship. He had never seen the West before and found it excitingly different. At dockside, he had his first look at the *Farragaut,* a sleek new destroyer, just finished refitting. Most of the ship's company was already there when he arrived. He was sure that a memorable time was ahead for all of them.

After a swift passage over the beautiful blue waters of the Pacific, they steamed into Pearl Harbor. Loren received his quarters assignment in the BOQ and settled in for his three-year tour of duty.

One of his fellow officers on the *Farragaut* was Marshall Lowell, whom he had known slightly at the Academy. Marsh had been a year ahead of Loren. When Loren entered the wardroom on the *Farragaut,* he hailed him. "Loren! Some of us get together for squash on the weekend. Do you play?"

"I played some at the academy, but I'm not very good."

"With one or two exceptions, we're not great players either. Why don't you come along? It's good exercise and a lot of fun."

"Sounds good. Tell me how to get there."

That Saturday, Marsh and he, and four others spent two hours at round robin matches at the court. Marsh, a classic endomorph, did not look like an athlete, but he was always in position to strike the ball when they played. He beat Loren easily in their thirty-minute slot.

As Loren was toweling off, Marsh came up to him. "Why don't you stop over for lunch? You can meet my wife."

"She won't mind an extra guest?"

"Not at all!"

Fifteen minutes later, the two men arrived at Marsh's house in the married housing area. As they tromped in the front door, Loren saw a tall, pretty young woman with blonde hair come from the back of the house.

"Loren, I'd like you to meet my wife, Gwen."

"I'm pleased to meet you," said Loren.

Gwen gave him a dazzling smile. "I'm very glad to meet you as well."

"Honey, I invited Loren for lunch."

"Well, if you give me a few minutes, I'll see what I can do."

Lunch at the Lowell's became a regular thing after squash. Loren decided to bring some wine for the occasion, and they talked about navy things as they ate. From the beginning, Gwen flirted with him.

Three months after he arrived in Hawaii, the *Farragaut* went to sea for combat exercises. Performing escort duty for the big battleships out from San Diego, the crew saw a lot of ocean. As signals officer, Loren had a busy but routine day-to-day and the time passed quickly.

Marsh, who liked to play cards, was always after Loren to get into the poker games when they were off duty, but Loren had no interest. He had taken the precaution of buying some books that he had wanted to read but hadn't found the time to do so. The *Farragaut* logged several thousand miles before returning to Pearl just before Christmas.

On a bright, sunny December morning, Loren walked down the street in downtown Honolulu. After three months at sea, he was glad to be back on dry land again. He needed to do some Christmas shopping. The females in his family would certainly appreciate pearl earrings for a gift, so he went to a jewelry store in downtown Honolulu that Gwen had recommended. He was holding an especially nice pair up to the light when he became aware that someone was watching him. He turned to see a lovely Japanese, elegantly dressed and coifed by his side. "She'll like that very much, Ensign."

"It's for my mother. Do you really think she will like it?"

"Absolutely. I have to go, now. Merry Christmas."

Loren laid the earrings on the counter. "I'll be back in a minute," he said to the clerk and turned to follow her. He was by her side in a moment. "Don't run off."

"I must go home, Ensign."

"You can't just drop into my life and then go away. Not until we have had a drink anyway."

She turned to look at him. "Just one, and then I really must go."

They talked for a half-hour or so in a hotel bar a short way from the store. He learned that Fumiko, or Fumi, was not a traditional Japanese. "We have a young set that pretty much goes around together to various parties, much to the chagrin of my father who is very conservative. If he knew that I was here with you now, he would have apoplexy." They laughed together. Besides being very pretty, she was charming and a good conversationalist, speaking English without a trace of an accent, and the time went by quickly. Suddenly, she looked at her watch. "I really have to go. Loren, it has been nice."

"Will you have dinner with me tomorrow night?"

Fumi looked into his eyes. "All right."

"Where can I call for you?"

"I'll meet you. I have my own car so it is not a problem. How about…here at seven?"

"I'll see you then."

They saw one another several times in the next few days and soon they were together whenever Loren's duties permitted. Because of the social attitudes of the peacetime navy, Loren did not take Fumi to any of the navy social affairs. He always went as a single, dancing with the older navy wives and being pleasant and sociable. As he had on many of these occasions, he saw Gwen and Marsh at a cocktail party.

Gwen was forever teasing him about his dark goings on off the base. "I know you have some sinful rendezvous out in the seamy part of Honolulu somewhere. I can just imagine the kind of things that…go on."

Loren and Marsh erupted in laughter. "Is she right, Loren? I could really use a change of pace."

"You two will be the first to know."

Gwen and Loren danced later in the evening. She clung to him as they whirled around the floor and, when the music stopped, she brushed his lips with a kiss as she looked into his eyes. She was beautiful and he was tempted, but she was his friend's wife. Loren was very diplomatic as he escorted her back to their table.

Loren and Fumi had dinner together again Saturday night. As they sipped their coffee, Fumi looked at him in a way that he could not read. "Loren, would you like to go swimming on the north shore tomorrow? My parents have a beach house up there."

"That sounds wonderful, Fumi. It would be nice to get away from the city for awhile."

"I'll pick you up outside the gate. How about ten?"

"I'll see you there."

Loren had a sense of well being, as Fumi and he drove through the pineapple and sugarcane plantations towards the north shore. Wearing a striped sailor shirt with white ducks, she was very fetching. Her dark, glossy hair rippled in the slight breeze from the open window.

"How much further, Fumi?"

"About another forty-five minutes. We'll be there soon."

As they neared their destination, a large, dark thundercloud developed over them. They pulled up to the beach house just as the rain began. With jackets over their heads, they dashed for the door. Inside, they turned to watch the torrent of rain raise dust clouds out on the dirt road. She turned to him and suddenly they were embracing. The warmth of her was overpowering.

Fumi reached for his hand. "Come with me."

They ascended the stairs to a large sleeping loft with a skylight. In seconds, they were out of their clothes and into the large feather bed. Her white skin, untouched by the sun, excited him as he caressed her.

Later, they lay spent on the bed. Loren reached for Fumi and drew her to him. Together they watched the rain spatter in crazy patterns on the skylight. He kissed her tenderly.

She dropped him at the main gate of the base. The rain had slackened and the overcast was breaking up. He held her in his arms. "This has been the finest day of my life, Fumi. I don't want it to end."

"We will have other days, Loren." Then they were embracing again.

The young lovers spent a glorious summer swimming in the surf on the north shore of Oahu. At night, they would go back to the beach house and make love between clean white sheets. Fumi would call her parents about staying overnight so they wouldn't be worried. It was an idyllic existence.

In the wardroom on the *Farragaut*, Loren's shipmates were wondering aloud about where he disappeared to on the weekends. "Come on," said Marsh, "own up. What are you up to, and does she have a friend?"

"I'm spending a lot of time at the beach. The body surfing is outstanding."

"I'll just bet." Loren remained close mouthed.

The *Farragaut* made ready for sea again in September for the scheduled naval maneuvers. At the dockside, Loren and Fumi said their goodbyes. "We're going to be gone awhile, Fumi. Probably about four months."

"I'll miss you, Loren."

"Will you be here when I get back?"

"Of course, silly!"

As he started up the gangway, Loren turned to wave. Fumi smiled as she raised her hand.

The maneuvers went well, and the *Farragaut* steamed back into port after a little over three months. Loren shouldered through the crowds toward the trim green LaSalle where Fumi waited for him. Then she was in his arms. Their embrace lasted a long time.

They resurrected the Saturday morning squash as well as lunch at the Lowell's. On the first weekend back, Gwen, Marsh and

Loren talked over club sandwiches. "Loren, you must come to our game night this Tuesday. We've really missed having you."

She sat across the table from him, never taking her eyes from him. Gwen was casually dressed in shorts and a short sleeved top. She seemed to glow in his presence.

Loren had been to the game nights regularly before the cruise. Their commanding officer, Bill Olds, was a sometimes guest. At the last one, Gwen had invited him to spend the night at their house because of the late hour.

Bill Olds chided him. "You should take her up on it, Loren. You never know what might result." The others laughed. There had been rumors of her relationship with their CO. Loren begged off, citing how he would frighten everyone without a shave the next morning.

Loren carried his dishes to the sink when they were finished as Gwen went to the back of the house.

"I'll drop you off if you are ready," said Marsh.

"Let me use your bathroom first and then we'll go."

"Right through that door and to the left."

Loren dried his hands and then walked out into the hall. The door to the bedroom was open. He was about to start toward the front of the house when Gwen walked by the open door. She did not look his way. She was completely nude. Shaken, Loren entered the living room where Marsh was waiting.

As Marsh stood up, Gwen entered the room, wearing a bright yellow sundress. "Well, Loren, can we count on you Tuesday?"

"I've got a date, Gwen." She was looking into his eyes again.

"Why don't you…rearrange your schedule. It's not like you have a steady or anything."

"I'm sorry, Gwen. I do have a date." She was cool toward him as he departed.

The *Farragaut* crew again settled into their shore duty routine. Loren received a promotion to Lieutenant Junior Grade and took on further responsibilities. There was always time for the navy social events and he was going to one that night, sporting his new half stripe. As usual, he went alone. One of his shipmates, Joe King, was there with his wife Mary. He knew the couple casually and went over to say hello. Mary greeted him, unsmiling, and in a short while led Joe away from where they were talking. Loren was at a loss. What could be bothering her? At the last affair, they had danced together and she was sunny and bright.

He found himself next to Joe King at the bar a short time later. Loren turned to him. "Do you have a minute, Joe?"

"Sure." They moved over next to some potted palms.

"Joe, what is it with Mary? She looked at me as though I was one of the local lepers."

Joe looked at him for a long moment. "I'd rather not say."

"Come on, Joe, what is it? If I've offended your family in any way, I'm sorry!"

"It's not that, Loren. It's just that everyone has heard about you and Gwen."

"What about Gwen and me?"

"How you pursued her and how she had to fight you off."

"That's not true, Joe! I never pursued her. If anything, it was the other way around!"

"That's not how she's telling it."

Loren looked hard at him. "Joe, it's just not so!"

"I didn't think you were that kind of guy, Loren. And people know that Gwen flits around a lot. Nevertheless, that's how it is."

On the bus back to his quarters, Loren thought about what Joe had told him. Then he knew what he had to do.

At a cocktail party given by the Captain, Loren arrived with Fumi on his arm. There was a notable stir as they entered. Loren made their introductions. Fumi was elegant and breathtakingly beautiful in a gray silk cocktail dress and a tasteful display of fine jewelry. There were many big-eyed wives as the couples talked over cocktails. Gwen was astounded and had little to say. Only Marsh was distant, taking his cue from Gwen.

Joe King was overwhelmed. "My God, Loren, where did you find her? She's striking!"

"We have been dating a long time."

Winter in Hawaii meant some warm rain showers, so Loren and Fumi continued to go to the north shore on the weekends, cavorting in the surf and enjoying loving afternoons in the cool shaded beachhouse. They were sleeping deeply in the loft when Loren suddenly started awake. He heard a door slam shut. Someone was in the house. Fumi stirred and looked at him. "There's someone downstairs, Fumi. I'll see what's going on."

He slipped on his terry beach robe before he started down the stairs. He came to the bottom and turned to see a short, well-muscled Japanese man. They stood staring at each other for a second.

"Who are you?" the man shouted with a strong accent. Loren heard Fumi's sharp intake of breath. "Father!"

Loren gathered himself. "I'm Lieutenant Loren Middleton, U.S. Navy. Your daughter was nice enough to let me spend the night here." The Japanese turned to Fumiko and berated her loudly in Japanese for some time as Loren stood helplessly by.

Then the man turned to him. "You will never see my daughter again!"

A flash of anger overtook Loren. "That's up to her!" He turned to Fumi. "Would you like to leave now?"

She found her voice. "In a minute." She turned away from them.

Her father screamed at him. "Get out of my house!"

"As soon as I get my gear." Loren walked past him and up the stairs.

Fumi was leaving the room just as he entered. There was fright in her eyes. "I will talk to him."

Loren dressed and came down the stairs. Fumi's father glared at him. Fumi stepped calmly between them. "We're going back to Honolulu now, Father." It was a quiet ride back to the city.

At the gate, he turned to her. "When will I see you?"

"Call me...tomorrow afternoon. Perhaps I will be able to make peace with him by then."

"I hope so, Fumi."

They talked on the phone the following afternoon. "Loren, my father has forbidden me to see you any more. He has threatened to send me to his brother in Nagoya if I disobey him."

"I'll talk to him, Fumi. I'll tell him about us. He'll understand."

"He will not listen, Loren. It is not just you. He hates all Caucasians."

Loren was at a loss. Finally, he spoke again. "Do we have to have his approval to be together? Can't we go on like we have been? He will see that it is all right eventually."

"Loren, I can't go against my family." A long silence followed.

"Then this is it, this is all there is."

"Yes, Loren." She paused. "I will miss you."

"I'll miss you, too, Fumi."

The metallic click of the circuit disconnecting echoed in his ears. He stared at the walls of the silent room. Then he rose from his chair and headed out the door.

CHAPTER VI—MTB

Loren's tour was almost over and HQ ordered him to start his checkout procedure. After three years, he was returning to the Continental United States and his next duty station. Loren found himself looking forward to his three years of shore duty in CONUS.

Dave Blackmon had told him about the newly forming Motor Torpedo Boat squadrons. "It's a brand new thing, Loren. There is a lot of room for advancement. You can get in on the ground floor."

"I take it you have applied?"

"You bet. It's the kind of thing I've been looking for."

"Who do I talk to?" Loren volunteered for the MTBs and his acceptance followed shortly thereafter.

When he returned to duty in San Diego in 1937, the Navy selected him to be part of the test team for the Higgins MTB. In the next year and a half, he would be testing the Higgins boat offshore in every kind of sea.

In going through his required reading, he found that the MTB was a radical departure from normal naval architecture. Built entirely of plywood with no armor at all, it relied on speed and maneuverability to elude enemy fire and perform its mission. Seventy feet long and twenty feet abeam, it could easily outrun any naval vessel afloat. The MTB, powered by three Packard engines with three screws, gave the boat captain the ability to command up to six thousand horsepower. These powerful, high performance engines needed changing out and complete overhaul every few hundred hours. With four torpedo tubes and two mounts of twin fifty caliber machine guns, Loren thought that the MTB would be a formidable opponent, at least in theory.

Their young commanding officer, Lt. Bainbridge, was in overall charge of the testing effort in San Diego. With the completion of the initial boat tests in the first six months, they were now concentrating on weapons trials. The project was slightly ahead of schedule.

The system that caused the most problems for Loren and the other boat captains was the compressed air launching of their torpedoes from the tubes. After several fruitless days, they had a skull session with the boat's engineers.

Lt. Bainbridge was plainly frustrated. "We have to get this thing working! We're now behind schedule instead of ahead of it. These boats are just so much plywood if we can't launch torpedoes."

One of the engineers spoke up. "I've been working on a mechanism that would just drop the torpedoes off the side, like a depth charge. It's not ideal, but I think it will work."

"We may have to fall back on something like that," said the Lieutenant.

The chief engineer spoke up. "We should stick by the original design and do what we have to do to make it work."

"I'll give you one more week, Joe. If it's still no go, we have to look at alternatives. Loren, work with Joe on this. Try to point out exactly what's happening."

"Yes, sir."

On the fifth day, they made a minor modification to the compressed air release mechanism and suddenly it was working. Loren and Joe celebrated noisily. "By God, we did it!" cried Joe.

"Never had a doubt," replied Loren with a grin.

The tube launcher was now more or less reliable, after a lot of on-site modifications. Happy with the outcome of the testing, Loren reflected on what was ahead. He believed that the true test of the MTBs would come in actual combat. With the events in Europe and the deteriorating conditions in the Far East, he thought it would not be long before he and his fellow officers, and their boats, would be involved in a real conflict. Because of this, the day-to-day testing activities were dynamic and exciting.

The cocktail party was just before the big dance at the hanger. Most of Loren's shipmates from the MTB testing effort were there as well as several other people.

Rod Somerlade came up to him as Loren was enjoying his first scotch on the rocks. "Loren, come with me a minute. I want to introduce you to someone."

"Lead on, Rod." They crossed the room toward a group in avid conversation. In the center of the group, wearing a white cocktail dress, was the most beautiful girl Loren had ever seen. Several young officers were talking all at once in an effort to impress her. Rod and Loren slipped by the cordon and he was face to face with her.

"Joyce, I'd like you to meet a shipmate of mine, Loren Middleton. Loren, this is my sister Joyce."

She gave him a dazzling smile as they exchanged greetings. The small combo in the corner started to play a dance tune. Joyce slipped her arm through his. "Shall we, Mr. Middleton?"

He held her close as they navigated the floor. She was the All-American Girl, with lovely blonde hair and green eyes. They talked briefly between numbers and then the combo started up again. Immediately, someone cut in and she danced away from him. She turned and smiled at him from the floor. Loren hoped he didn't look as overwhelmed as he felt. They danced again before the partygoers left for the big dance. With so many admirers clustered around Joyce, Loren was not certain who her date was.

Loren called her the following day and made a date for the movies that weekend. He learned that she was twenty and attending college, majoring in child development. He met her parents when he called for her.

Mrs. Somerlade offered her hand. "It's nice to meet you, Mr. Middleton. In these times, I'm glad that people like you and Rod are serving our country. We're going to need you, I'm afraid, before long."

"I'm happy to meet you as well, Mrs. Somerlade. I hope that this mess overseas can be settled without Rod and I having to go off to fight someone. We are ready, however."

At that moment, Joyce descended the stairs, smiling. Loren had that feeling in the pit of his stomach again. "Hello, Joyce."

"Mr. Middleton."

"Are we ready to go?"

"As soon as I get my wrap."

They saw a lot of each other in the next few weeks. Though nothing formal existed between them, everyone understood that they were together. He was tall, considered handsome, and had, in the opinion of many, a promising career ahead of him. Girls had always liked Loren and he liked the idea that Joyce had chosen him out of many others as her beau. They went everywhere together and Loren enjoyed showing her off at the many navy functions that young officers attended.

Her beauty raised a natural passion in him, but it was strictly hands off with Joyce. Some moderate necking and a kiss at the door were all that he enjoyed of her. His level of frustration grew as the spring moved into summer. Loren felt like they were never alone. Besides the social set that Joyce was a part of, eager young Naval Officers were always hanging around the fringes of their group. Sometimes, Loren felt like he was living in a fishbowl.

They returned from the dance late in the evening. Loren pulled up next to a wooded area just below her house. Joyce looked at him but said nothing. Then, suddenly, they were kissing as his hands roamed her body. He unzipped her dress and then reached behind her to unfasten her bra. It came away easily, revealing lovely, rose-tipped breasts.

As he touched her, she started and then pulled away. "Loren, No! We can't!" Her flushed face and shining eyes betrayed her excitement.

In an effort to regain his composure, Loren breathed in deeply. "All right, Joyce."

She pulled her bra down and attempted to fasten it. "Will you help me, Loren?" He could smell her hair as he refastened her bra. "Will you walk me to the door?"

"Of course." He held her close to him as they crossed the street.

As they stood on her porch, she looked into his eyes. "This has been such a wonderful time, Loren. I wish we could be together like this for always." Then she melted into his arms.

When they talked on the phone the following day, she seemed as cool and calm as ever. "I liked being with you last night. I'm only human, but I want someone who is going to be there for me always before I let my emotions take over completely."

"I understand. We need to talk. I'll call you Friday. We're going to be testing all week."

"All right, darling. Till then."

Loren thought about Joyce afterward. He was in a bad way in his want of her. He considered whether the time had come for his bachelor days to be over. He could never find a finer girl for his wife than Joyce and he wanted her desperately. Anyway, they would talk about it Friday.

The current phase of MTB Operational Testing was finishing up. Loren expected to have his tour extended for the next testing phase. Unexpectedly, he received orders to one of the first MTB squadrons that were forming up for overseas duty.

Dave Blackmon sought him out. "Loren, I've been ordered to one of the overseas squadrons. Somebody said you had too."

"That's right. I understand that with the international situation being what it is, especially in the Far East, the Navy wants experienced MTB squadrons on the spot. By the way, you and I are going to be in the same squadron."

"Really! That's great. Looking forward to it."

"Me too. The next question is, where will we be sent?"

"We'll find out soon enough."

With Loren's new assignment came a promotion to full Lieutenant and a billet as Executive Officer of the squadron. He was also captain of one of the new Higgins boats. Their newly formed squadron, consisting of six boats and their crews, received orders to report for duty in the Philippines.

Joyce and Loren went to the movies Friday night. Afterwards, they parked in front of her house. She glanced at him momentarily, but said nothing.

He turned to her in the front seat. "Joyce, I've received orders to the Philippines. We will be leaving very soon."

Joyce looked at him again. "I thought you might be. Rod just received orders for Newport News, Virginia. They're forming an MTB squadron there." She looked away. "Loren, what about us?"

"That's what I wanted to talk to you about. I'd like you to come with me."

"To the Orient?"

"Yes."

"Is this a proposal?"

"Yes, it is, Joyce. You know how I feel about you."

"I feel the same way, Loren. Does it have to be the Philippines?"

"You go where the Navy sends you."

"Isn't there something you can do? Someplace like Newport News would be really nice."

"I could ask, but I know what the answer will be."

"Loren, I don't want to go to some wild place thousands of miles away where there's no one I know."

"A lot of wives are doing it."

"My family and my friends are here, Loren. Can't we be married and I'll be here for you when you get back?"

"I'm going to be gone three years, Joyce!"

She was quiet for a moment. "No, I guess that wouldn't work out, would it?"

"No. I thought you loved me, Joyce."

"I do."

"But not that much?"

"I'm sorry, Loren."

"So am I, Joyce."

CHAPTER VII—THE OCEAN CRUISE

That all seemed long ago now, as he watched the crew securing the last of the fuel drums on the deck of the 25 boat. His thoughts returned to the present as he went through his mental checklist. Yes, they were finally ready, ready to head out into the unknown.

At 2100, the heavily loaded 25 boat moved away from her pier and headed down channel. In an hour, they were out in the open sea, steering well west of the normal shipping lanes. The rough sea broke heavily across their bow, but the fuel drums they had lashed to the deck stayed in place. Loren, Dave, and Dave's exec, Ensign Tom Kite, took turns conning the boat as they raced toward the south. Twenty-foot waves came over the cockpit, soaking everyone on deck to the skin. They were cold and miserable. The rough seas caused them to swing wildly back and fourth across the course they attempted to hold. At least they were on the open sea, with no major obstacles to worry about, for the present. With Tom at the conn, Loren and Dave struggled with the navigation charts belowdecks as the boat pitched and rolled.

Loren called out to Jess Roe as Dave and he tried to remain upright. "Jess, have a look at our hull and see if we're holding together. You'd better do it every half hour or so until we get out of these heavy seas."

"Roger, Skipper." Jess headed forward.

The others not directly involved in operating the MTB found niches where they could be as comfortable as possible and not be knocked around in the cabin. JoAnne and Beverly, wrapped in a blanket, clung together. A tired crew looked forward to the daylight hours when they would have time to rest.

Loren and Dave had previously planned their first landfall in some small islands in the northern part of the Sulu Sea. The islands, surrounded by reefs, had lagoons so shallow that a destroyer could not enter. Their MTB needed only five feet of water to float and to clear their rudders, struts and propellers.

They had planned an ETA of 0400 to allow for possible delays in their transit. Things went exceptionally well and he and Dave sighted the islands while they were still in darkness. Loren, at the conn, cruised slowly along the shoreline, looking for an anchorage. After about half an hour, he spotted the mouth of a stream, with banks overgrown with tropical vegetation and overhanging trees.

"There! We couldn't find a better place if we looked all day." They anchored in the streambed close to the bank, and a work party set about immediately cutting palm fronds to camouflage the boat's hull. In forty minutes, the boat, now effectively hidden, was almost undetectable, even on the surface. Then the exhausted voyagers found a bunk or a mattress on the deck and slept soundly. Loren and Don Buchman, the Marine, took the first watch ashore.

A little after noon, people started to stir. Loren, who had managed a little sleep, called them all together. "OK, listen up! We don't know if these islands are occupied or not, so the word is silence. Sound will carry miles in this situation. Ensign Kite will form a work party to unlash some of the fuel drums and pour the gas into our tanks. While he is doing this, all electric devices must be off and the smoking lamp is definitely out. That aviation gas is so volatile it could blow us to kingdom come.

"Everyone else who is not on shore watch, stay on the boat unless it's a call of nature. When on shore, don't go any place by yourself. One of the shore guards can act as an escort. Bury everything! Don't leave any garbage lying around to show the Japs that we've been here. Tom, you need to sink the empty fuel drums in deep water.

"Ramon, when Ensign Kite finishes, get some chow underway and we'll eat and rest up for tonight."

The repast was very basic, as Ramon had only an electric hotplate to work with. The part time cooks from the two boats pitched in to help and after lunch everyone rested, getting ready for what was to come. Loren went topside and sat on one of the empty torpedo tubes. In a few minutes, JoAnne came up to join him. For the first time since they were preparing to leave the cove, they had a chance to talk.

"Hi, JoAnne."

"Hello. How are you holding up?"

"I'm tired."

"You should try to get some more sleep before tonight."

"I thought I'd stretch out on the deck for awhile. How's Bev?"

"She's better today, although she's still withdrawn. Of course, she was never very outgoing."

"I guess part of it is her upbringing. Esky told me that her parents were missionaries in China until the Japanese forced them out. I don't think she approves of a lot of things she's seen."

"I didn't know that." She was silent for a minute. "Loren, I'm so glad to be here with you."

He touched her hand. "I'm glad too."

Loren wondered if the Japs had missed them and were mounting an air search trying to find them. They saw an aircraft far away on the horizon that afternoon and assumed it was Japanese.

At 2100, the 25 boat pulled away from its anchorage and out into the shallow waters of the bay. Dave had the conn, while Loren and Tom set up the chart for navigation. In twenty minutes, they were out into the open sea and traveling at high speed toward the south. The weather was better and the sea a lot smoother than the night before. Their passage was uneventful and the island they had selected to spend the daylight hours hove into view as a dark shadow at 0330. The Packard engines had not missed a beat.

Loren looked in vain for some kind of landmark in the dark, as he ran slowly parallel to the white surf breaking in the distance. Only the mountainous profile of the island stood out against the overcast sky. He considered rigging a sea anchor so that they could stand off the coast until it got lighter. He was about to get someone started on it when suddenly a large floodlight blinked on. The beam moved back and forth looking for them.

He whispered urgently to Tom. "Get those guns manned!"

Tom disappeared below decks and, in seconds, two gunners ran to their turrets. At that instant, the searchlight caught them in a harsh, bright light and gun flashes emanated from the shore. Loren wheeled the boat ninety degrees and firewalled the throttle. The 25 boat leapt forward. "Knock out that light!" he shouted.

The fifty calibers opened up as huge explosions and large geysers of water erupted around them. They had been within point blank range of the beach and were now desperately trying to run from the intense barrage. One of the gunners spun away from his mount, hit by shrapnel. The other twin 50 mount continued to hammer away and suddenly the searchlight went out. Loren changed course immediately and continued to run at flank speed. The action was over in less than five minutes.

Alone on the bridge, Loren watched with dismay as the sky lightened in the East. Then Dave came up and peered at the horizon. "Any sign of our alternate landfall?"

"Not yet."

"I'm glad we planned for an alternate. The only problem is, the Japs might be there too."

"The Japs know we're here and their air patrols will be searching for us. Unless we anchor in an area with some cover very soon, the Japanese will find us and sink us." The two men scanned the ocean in desperation.

The sun was well above the horizon when Loren spotted the low-lying island chain. "There! To the southeast!"

"I see them. Let's go!"

Loren piloted the 25 boat at high speed toward the islands, hoping that no reefs were in his path. He saw a small stream emptying into the sea on the second island. Loren cut back on his speed in the shallows and the boat glided toward the dense greenery of the stream bank. The sluggish stream was barely moving. Dave was searching the sky for enemy aircraft.

When they had anchored, the camouflage crew worked with desperate urgency, disguising the MTB so that it was not visible from the sea or especially from the air. They finished camouflaging the craft and finally had time to rest. About fifteen minutes later, the men and women aboard the MTB heard the drone of an aircraft engine. The Jap seaplane was flying a pattern over a large area, looking for them. They watched it through the trees as it methodically flew back and forth. No one spoke a word. After about twenty minutes, the plane flew on down the island chain.

The gunner from Dave's crew who had manned one of the twin .50 mounts was dead. They made preparations to bury him at sea that night. Ron Vanolli, the other gunner from Loren's crew, had a flesh wound in his upper arm.

Bev had dressed the wound and was taking Ron's temperature when Loren went below. "How are you doing, Ron?"

"Just fine, Skipper," the handsome young Italian replied with a smile. "It's only a little nick."

Loren looked at Bev. "How is he, Lieutenant?"

"He'll be OK," she replied, without looking at him. A subdued group went about their daytime routine and prepared for the night. They emptied the last of the fuel drums into the MTB's tanks.

Ramon came to him after they had eaten that afternoon. "What are your plans after reaching Mindanao, sir?"

"Why do you ask?"

"My village is up in the mountains of northern Mindanao. If we could reach there, we would be safe, at least for now."

Loren reflected on this. "Tell me more."

They talked for about a half-hour and then broke out the naval charts. Ramon showed him the approximate location of his village. The charts showed an inlet on the coast that was reasonably close.

Loren pointed to the map. "Do you know this place on the coast?"

"Yes, it's the closest to where we would be going."

"Is there any cover?"

"No, it's a rocky shoreline."

Loren called Dave and Tom over to the chart table and explained what Ramon was proposing.

Dave checked the chart. "That inlet is down the coast a ways. We are going to be short of fuel."

Loren went over his numbers again. "Based on our consumption so far, we should have enough to make it. We would have to debark in a hurry and probably scuttle the boat before it gets light."

They went on to discuss the details of the proposed plan. "We're going to have to remove the radio equipment and transport it to our destination," said Loren. "It's going to be heavy and unwieldy, but it's our only link with the outside world."

Ramon spoke up. "Lieutenant, it's not that far to my village, but it's a long, hard climb to get there."

"We'll take that into account, Ramon. We don't have much choice."

Loren called everyone together late that afternoon and told them about the plan. The others had no dissenting views to offer, so they started their preparations for the evening's run.

Loren was dead tired as he stretched out on the narrow mattress next to the torpedo tube. The sun was still high in the sky and he knew that he had to get some rest to be ready for the night. The adrenaline was flowing from the frantic events of the night before. Still, he felt good about the last two days and his part in it, despite the lone casualty. Now he would lead his small command to safety at last, away from the battlefield of Bataan.

CHAPTER VIII—THE VILLAGE

On the deck of the MTB, Loren started awake as a hand touched his shoulder. Thomas was kneeling next to him, a thatch of red hair covering his forehead. "It's time, Skipper. We have to start getting ready." At dusk, they headed for the open sea.

They passed through the narrow entrance to the Mindanao Sea and on toward their destination. At 0430, they sighted the rocky inlet on the coast of Mindanao. Loren got as close as he could to the beach and dropped anchor.

He addressed the crew. "OK, let's unload our gear on the beach. Be careful of the radio! It's our only link to the outside." Loren looked at the large green hill in front of them. "It looks like we don't have any cover for quite a ways. Dave, get our gear up in the greenery as fast as you can. Ensign Kite, are you up to a good long swim?"

"As ready as I'll ever be."

"You and I will take the boat out to the center of the cove and sink her."

The crew began to unload the MTB, wading in chest deep water. Day was breaking when they deposited the last of their gear on the narrow beach. The radio had been particularly hard to manage. Loren and Tom restarted the engines and pulled out into the deep part of the inlet. They killed the engines and opened the seacocks. As the sea began to wash over the decks, the two officers dove into the water and started their long swim ashore.

On the beach, Dave sent a work party up to the tropical forest that ended a mile from the shore. They were looking for bamboo trunks and anything else that they could use to help transport the sizable amount of supplies on the beach. In an hour, they had fashioned some crude slings. The pickets that Dave posted were scanning the landscape for any evidence of activity. Ready at last, they moved off the beach and headed for the edge of the verdant forest, their heavy burdens biting into their shoulders.

They rested in the gloom of the forest while Ramon and Tom went to reconnoiter. Loren reflected that so far they had been extraordinarily lucky. The men were back in a half-hour. Ramon motioned back from where they had come. "There is a jungle trail heading in the right direction, sir. It will be hard going with all of these supplies. There is also a small fishing village just over that hill."

"OK, let's get going. We'll see how we do." They shouldered their burdens again and headed up the slope. After about two hours, the exhausted crew stopped for a rest. The men were soaked to the skin in the oppressive heat and humidity. Swarms of insects buzzed around them, looking for exposed skin. Apparently, they would have to find another way to get their supplies to Ramon's village.

Dave lay back against a rock, breathing deeply. "We could cache this stuff off the trail somewhere. No one would ever find it and we could come back for it later."

Ramon turned to Loren. "When we get to the village, we could send a cart back on the road and load it up at night."

"Wouldn't that be dangerous?"

"Only if the Japanese search us. Our people will be willing to take the chance."

"As much as I hate risking your Filipinos, Ramon, that is probably the best way. We Americans are going to have to stay out of sight or we'll have Japs crawling all over us."

"I'll go to the village to see what information I can pick up." Ramon sloughed off his pack and headed back up the trail. The others set about caching the supplies.

Loren spoke to the company. "Use your ponchos to wrap everything. It's important to keep things dry, especially the radio. I know it's been built to military specs and all, but getting it doused with rain water probably wouldn't do it any good."

They were still working on the cache when Ramon returned. "The news is not good. The Japanese have occupied this part of Mindanao, though there aren't that many of them. They patrol regularly, but they are spread thin."

"We need to get going as soon as possible then."

While they were working, Gunner's Mate 2nd Class Thomas organized and issued a survival kit for each of them. JoAnne made sure that each of them carried essential medical supplies, such as halozone tablets to purify their water and quinine to combat malaria. At length, they got underway again. The crew ate their rations cold that evening, because even a small fire would risk detection.

Loren spoke to the crew before they turned in. "Have a good look at where you are bedding down. There's nothing worse than to discover in the middle of the night that you are sleeping on top of an anthill! We'll mount a watch to keep an eye out for marauding wildlife as well as for Japs. We'll get started at daybreak." Cold and uncomfortable in the night, they slept as best they could on the trail.

The crew started early the next morning, climbing the steep terrain into the green jungle. They had been on the trail about two hours when the rains came. With no ponchos to protect them, everyone was soon soaking wet. They crossed their first stream and found that some of them had acquired leeches on their lower bodies. The smokers among them lit cigarettes and applied them to the clinging bloodsuckers. Loren, who did not smoke, borrowed Dave's cigarette for the task. Despite their precautions, the first cases of dysentery started to appear. At JoAnne's insistence, Loren cautioned everyone again about purifying their drinking water.

Late on the second day, Ramon came to Loren. "My village is just over the next hill, Lieutenant. We are almost there!"

"I'll be glad to see it, Ramon."

Dirty, tired and bedraggled they trooped into his village just as the sun was going down. Ramon spoke with the village elders for some time, telling them about who the Navy men were and why they were there. The villagers showed them to their new quarters individually, with elaborate courtesy. Ramon invited Loren to his home. When Loren entered, Ramon introduced him to his wife. She looked about forty, small and very pleasant. Three young children stood watching him, a girl and two boys whose names Ramon rattled off.

"Oh, and here is my daughter Thomasina. We call her Tomi."

Loren turned to acknowledge her and stared for a moment, struck by her beauty. His hand went instinctively to the stubble on his face. Their eyes met for a second and then she looked down.

"Hello, Tomi," he managed.

"It is an honor to have you in our house, Lieutenant. We thank you for saving our father's life." Her English was impeccable.

"Did you tell them I took a shot at you?" Loren asked Ramon with a tired smile.

"I omitted that part."

Tomi came toward him. "Please follow me, Lieutenant, and I will show you where you can rest." He watched her as she moved with infinite grace ahead of him. Tomi showed him his room and the sleeping roll he would use. He thanked her, and the sliding door closed. She had not looked up again. He stripped his dirty uniform away and stretched out on the down filled pad. In seconds, he was asleep.

Loren awoke well rested and refreshed but badly in need of a bath. A knock sounded and Ramon opened the sliding door. "Good morning, Lieutenant. I hope you slept well."

"Good morning, Ramon. What happened to my uniform?"

"I took the liberty of having it washed for you. I brought this for you to wear until it is ready." Ramon gave him a sari-like garment that covered him from his waist to his ankles.

"I really need to get cleaned up, Chief."

"There's a stream about a quarter mile into the forest where you can bathe. Here in the village, we have no running water." Loren gratefully took the homemade soap that Ramon offered and headed for the stream. He was feeling better still a half-hour later as he returned to the village. Tomi had seen him coming and wordlessly presented him with a small box. As he took it, he looked at her. Their eyes met again and, this time, she returned his gaze. When he opened the box, he found a straight razor and a strop.

Clean-shaven, Loren joined Ramon in the dining area of his home. Tomi and Ramon's wife served them an early lunch, the females never dining with the males of the family. Loren was ravenous. After he had eaten, he went outdoors and found several of his crew in various stages of cleaning up. The sun shone brightly and the mountain air was invigorating.

JoAnne and Beverly were just returning from the communal stream when he ran into them. JoAnne was the picture of happiness and contentment as she talked about their experiences in the village so far. "Oh, yes, we have really nice quarters. Isn't this mountain air marvelous? Bev and I must have slept twelve hours. Bathing in that stream is quite an experience. I still have goose bumps!"

"I'm glad you're settled in. We'll relax for a day or so before we get organized. How are you doing, Bev?"

"I'm fine!"

Bev, for the first time in quite awhile, had some color in her cheeks as she smiled at him. She was very pretty in an unusual way, with her pale glowing complexion and dark soft hair.

Loren spent part of the afternoon walking the perimeter of Ramon's village. The thatched houses of the village were in a large bowl and built at ground level rather than on stilts like those on the seacoast. Dirt paths ran between the various buildings. Mountains and dark green forests surrounded them and he saw only one road in. It would be easily defensible if it ever came to that. He decided to call an officer's meeting the next morning to discuss their situation.

Loren, Dave, and Tom got together on a green knoll overlooking the road into the village as the sun rose above the horizon. Tom, an R.O.T.C. graduate from the University of Wisconsin, was new to the Navy but had shown good presence of mind during the escape. He was of medium height, slim, with boyish looks and a slightly ruddy complexion. Loren listened to what he had to say and he noticed that Dave, who was also from the Academy, did as well.

Loren spoke first. "I thought we should get together to discuss where we're going, now that we've got out of Bataan. I've been thinking a lot about just what our potential as a group is here on Mindanao. We are only a few men with a very modest armory. I don't see us taking back Mindanao or even shooting the Japs up, at least not for any length of time." The others agreed. "I also don't think that trying to link up with the U.S. military here is a viable thing to do.

From what Ramon was able to piece together, what there is of the U.S. presence is far to the south of us. I don't think we could hope for more than being assigned to another Naval Battalion anyway."

"Well, what do you think we should do," Tom asked, "sit around here and wait until our troops come back?"

"No, we need to pursue an active role against the Japanese."

"There's probably some other irregulars up in the hills," offered Dave. "They're probably mostly Filipino. We could try to link up with them."

"I think we should do that, Dave. I'll talk to Ramon. Our first priority had better be getting our gear and supplies up here, however. We need to see if we can establish contact with the outside world on our radio. Our codebooks are probably obsolete by now, but they still might work. Let's see what we can get going in that area. Dave, will you take charge of that?"

"Roger, Skipper."

"I had an idea that we could function like a Coastwatcher group. We could determine size, strength and disposition of enemy forces and communicate it to our people."

"Yeah!" Dave replied. "That might be harder to implement than it sounds, however."

"I'll come up with a plan and we can discuss this further." They talked some more about general topics and then trooped back down the hill to the village.

CHAPTER IX—TOMI

Loren called an all hands meeting for later in the afternoon. He explained that they were looking at their options. "We are putting together a plan. When it's complete, we'll present it. I want to encourage everyone to offer suggestions if they have them. Let's make the best of what we have."

After the meeting, he returned to Ramon's house. Still mentally tired from the past few days, he lay back on his sleeping pallet and closed his eyes. Something caused him to awake. He listened for a moment, but all was quiet except for the sound of trickling water. He arose and slid back his door. As he walked down the hallway, he glanced at the half open door to his right. Tomi was standing by a basin on her dresser, sponging off. She was totally nude. Loren stood transfixed, not able to take his eyes from her. She turned her head slightly and saw him in the doorway. Their eyes held for long seconds. Then she turned gracefully, took a light silk robe from a hanger, and donned it. Loren strode down the hallway and then outside, hitting his head on the low doorway as he did. In the bright sunshine outside, he swallowed hard and breathed deeply.

That evening, Tomi was especially attentive to him as Ramon and he had their evening meal. He looked at her and she smiled. She said nothing.

The next morning, Dave and a party of three sailors accompanied by Ramon started down the jungle trail to the cache.

Three men from the village started an hour later down the dusty road, driving a two wheeled cart pulled by a water buffalo, which the villagers called a carabao. Loren dined alone that evening, as Tomi and Ramon's wife served him.

About midnight, a soft knock at his door awakened him. The door slid noiselessly open and Tomi entered his room, wearing a beautiful white robe. He started to say something, but Tomi quieted him with a finger to her lips. She let the robe fall to the floor. For a space of time, he could do nothing but look at her exquisite nakedness. Then he reached out his hand to her. In a moment, she was under the bedcovers of his pallet and in his arms. Loren kissed her lovingly as he explored her body. He held back momentarily as he entered her, astonished to find a physical barrier. Then they made love easily, slowly.

When they lay together afterwards, she spoke to him in a low voice. "Now we are really as one," she said in her perfect, cultured English. "Did you know that there is an opera about people like us, the handsome naval officer and the exotic oriental woman?" He quieted her with a loving kiss on her lips. They clung together as he held her in his arms.

They stole moments together in the dead of night. After their lovemaking, they talked in low voices about their lives and the things that had meaning for each of them.

He cradled her in his arms as he touched her dark, shining hair. "You speak English so perfectly! How did you learn?"

"I went to a Catholic Mission school in Cagayen. All of our classes were taught in English."

"I've been trying to learn the local dialects but it's been a struggle."

"I will help you if that is what you want."

"Thank you. I very much want to learn." Then, in the dark, they loved again.

Dave returned two days later, followed closely by the creaking two wheeled cart with their radio and supplies hidden under a load of hay. The next days were long ones as Loren and Dave, with the help of Torpedoman Second Class Rod Wells, labored to get their radio working. Rod, who had been a part time radio technician as a civilian, was a torpedoman because that was what the Navy needed at that particular time. Handsome and personable, he worked well with the others.

On the following Monday, Ramon took Loren aside. "Lieutenant, I need to talk to you. I want you to know that I understand about you and Tomi."

Loren was taken aback. "You know? Are you sure that it's all right? I want you to know that Tomi is very special to me."

"She has told me about how it is between you. I am happy for both of you."

The two men shook hands. "Thank you, Ramon. Thank you for understanding."

Afterwards, Loren thought about what had happened. Tomi's mother must have told him about them. He realized that she had probably known about them from the beginning and perhaps had encouraged their relationship. That evening, when he went to the back of the house, he found the furnishings changed so that Tomi and he were sharing a room.

The following morning, he awoke early. The gray light of dawn was barely visible as he lay back on their pallet. He looked at the beautiful young girl, asleep at his side. He had not had a serious relationship since Joyce, and they had gone their separate ways over two years ago. He examined his own motives, regarding Tomi. Was this just a wartime thing, brought on by the precariousness of their day-to-day existence, or was it something deeper? He had the tenderest of feelings for her. At that moment, he wanted to take her in his arms. No, this was not just a wartime thing. He wondered where it would all lead.

The radio became operational ten days later and they transmitted their first tentative inquiries. They kept their transmissions short because of their fear of detection. In what had become the radio shack, the men talked about the problem. Loren sat looking at the radio. "Obviously, we have to develop a different method of transmitting information. Does anyone have any ideas?"

Rod Wells spoke up. "I've got one that might work, sir. The two-wheeled cart is the place to install the radio. With battery power, it's mobile. It would be harder to zero in on the location of the transmission if it's different every time."

Dave took it a step further. "We can install a key on the footboard of the cart. The driver of the cart could key in messages by sending with his foot as the wagon rolls along." These two options became part of their normal operations.

In the meantime, Machinist's Mate Jess Roe was working diligently, trying to build a recharging system for the radio batteries. He was using the engine and generator from an ancient bus that no longer ran to develop the capability. After several days, Scott and he reported to Loren. "We've got the engine running now, sir. Setting up the generator should be pretty straightforward."

Loren smiled a tired smile. "That's good. Now we should be able to recharge the radio's batteries for as long as they last."

In an attempt to find out if other bands of irregulars were operating in their vicinity, Ramon had gone on foot to the fishing village they had passed on their way up the mountain. When he returned, he went to Loren.

"What did you find out, Ramon?"

"There are no guerrilla groups here in this part of Mindanao. You know, there are very few people and very few Japanese as well. This might change if more Japanese come. Most of the people I talked to had not even seen a Japanese."

"Well, Ramon, it looks like we are on our own."

"Yes, it does."

With Tomi in their room that night, he thought about what Ramon had said. Whatever the naval contingent was going to do, they would be doing it without outside help.

They received their first reply from a military transmitter far to the west, requesting that they identify themselves. Their codebooks were still good! Loren keyed in a message they had prepared for this eventuality. In it he gave his name and rank, and briefly described their situation. Some time passed before they heard again.

When the reply came, Rod let out a whoop. "Wow! We got through!"

Dave was excited as well. "That's terrific! Now, they know we're here!"

"That they do," said Loren. "Tom, we'd better set up a meeting to tell the men."

"I'll get right on it."

In an all hands meeting later that day, Loren told the others about their good fortune, though most of them had heard already. "It's time for all of us to get organized toward obtaining information that can be transmitted to our radio contact in the U.S. military. Tom, to start things off I'd like you to organize a party to go down the jungle trails to the south and determine how far the Japanese have penetrated on Mindanao. We'll get one of Ramon's villagers to act as your guide."

"Roger, Skipper." They left the following morning with provisions for four days.

Amid the frantic activity, Loren and Tomi found time for themselves. When their door closed in the evening, their time together was enchanted. They could not get enough of each other, with sweet tender love again and again. Tomi patiently drilled him on the native dialects and his vocabulary grew rapidly. Soon, he could hold a conversation with her in Visayan or Tagalog. She could not do enough for him and he, in turn, had never been so happy in all his life.

One evening, as he was doing writing exercises in Visayan, he noticed her watching him. "What, Tomi?"

"How old are you, Loren?"

He chuckled. "Ancient. I'm thirty."

She looked perplexed. "And you are not married?"

"No. Why do you ask?"

"In the Philippines, people marry when they are much younger. It's not that way in America?"

"A lot of people there marry when they are quite young. I've just never found the right person. It's hard when you are in the Navy. You have to move around a lot. Some people don't like to live like that." He thought of Joyce.

"I see. When this war is over, I would like us to be married."

"I would like that too, Tomi."

Ramon's prestige among the villagers had grown since he had the leader of the naval contingent living at his house. With a quiet sense of pride, his wife told the village wives that Loren had taken Tomi as his woman. The rumor eventually spread to the naval personnel. No one said anything, but Loren noticed some of the crew looking at him questioningly.

Loren talked to Tomi about it. "We need to let people know about us, Tomi. I think the rumor mill is running overtime."

"What can we do, Loren?"

"Maybe take a walk through the village together?"

"When would you like to do this?"

"Tomorrow at noon?"

"I'll be ready, Loren."

At noon the next day, they walked hand in hand down the main pathway. The loving look they had for each other erased all doubt. JoAnne seemed surprised and was reluctant to talk about it when he spoke to her afterwards. Everyone else seemed to see the situation with no apparent concern and they all pressed on with the accelerated level of activity.

Loren led the next mission to the north to determine the strength and dispositions of the Japanese troops in their area, with Ramon as his guide. While he was in the field, Tom Kite and his team returned with much data. Dave started to generate the report they would transmit to U.S. HQ.

Loren lay close to the ground in the tangled greenery as he examined the periphery of the main Japanese base. The ever-present insects hummed in the foliage. The villagers concocted a vile smelling insect repellent from the bark of certain trees that protected him from the worst of the damage. He continually had to discipline himself against slapping mosquitoes on his exposed skin because, in the silence of the night, the sound would be as sharp as a gunshot.

He counted six tanks, lined up in a row and heavily guarded. He looked for Radio Direction Finding trucks but saw none. For the time being, at least, the Japanese did not appear to have RDF equipment to locate their transmissions. Counting the number of barracks gave him a good idea of their troop strength. He knew that Ramon was perusing the Japanese dispositions on the opposite side from where he was. When he observed all that he could, he crawled stealthily back into the dense, dank jungle. When he rendezvoused with Ramon and Mike Hanson, who acted as their focal point, he and

Ramon spoke in a combination of Tagalog and Visayan. Loren was increasingly fluent in the Philippine dialects, thanks to Tomi.

Mike's job was to give them cover if the Japs pursued them. He had one of the Thompsons and grenades clipped to his pack straps. After they exchanged information on what they had seen, they retreated up the trail in the dark of night. When they returned to the village, they brought with them a wealth of information to add to Dave's report.

Loren looked over the sizeable amount of data they had collected. "I think it's time to try to send this information out."

Dave spoke up. "I'm ready whenever you are."

"I thought I would take this on, Dave."

"You're too tall to pass for a Filipino. Ramon can find me some farmer's clothes and with my straw hat and a little stain from the bark of the local trees, I'll do just fine."

"You've got it then. What about the radio?"

"I'll have Wells hide in the load of hay. He'll operate the radio and read the message aloud to me so I can key it in on the floorboard. We won't begin transmission until we are some distance away from the village. I figure that we will be back at the end of the second day."

"Sounds like you've got it all figured out. Good luck and we'll see you when you get back."

In the night, Loren held Tomi in his arms and told her of his love for her. She responded to their lovemaking naturally and with pleasure. She was angry with him only when he took steps to see that she not get pregnant, even though he was thinking of her. He finally gave in to her remonstrations, though he knew what the inevitable result would be.

In their sixth month together, she came to him. "Loren, I am with child."

He went to her and held her close. "That's wonderful, Tomi. You'll be a fine mother. I love you so much."

Inwardly, his reaction to the news was one of apprehension. My God, he thought, what if the Japanese should come when she was in an advanced state of pregnancy, or, worse yet, with an infant? They had to have a plan to make sure that didn't happen. He'd have to think of what was best for them to do. Until then, they would be vulnerable.

In the first few days of the new year, Japanese patrols increased noticeably. When Loren's team went back to the Japanese army camp, they saw that the enemy had increased their presence considerably, including multiple RDF units. As they retreated back to the mountains, they narrowly escaped discovery by a patrol.

Loren discussed the situation with his officers when he returned. "We're going to have to take a lot more care now. To start with, we had better not have anyone leaving the village without an armed escort. We had also better plan what we are going to do if the Japs come up that road. Buchman has volunteered to train a fire team with the BAR as the centerpiece, Marine style. That will be a good start." They agreed to meet the next day with some more concrete proposals. Loren passed the word at an all hands meeting he had called later that day.

After the meeting, Ramon took him aside. "I'm worried about Tomi. Before long, she will not be able to travel the jungle trails to escape the Japanese because of the child."

"I know. What do you propose we do?"

"I have a sister who lives in a village about fifty kilometers from here. Tomi would be safe there. I will take her."

"I'll talk to her."

"No, I won't go! I want to be here with you." She was adamant.

"I want to be with you too, but what if the Japanese come, say two or three months from now? You would probably be killed, you and our child."

She was silent. At length, she replied. "You are right. When I think of our baby, I know you are right. I will go." She looked down and would not meet his eyes.

"Your parents think you should go, too. It won't be for long."

They said their goodbyes the next morning as Ramon readied the cart and carabao for the trip. Tomi was quiet and subdued. He held her close for a long while and then helped her up to the seat next to her father. Loren watched the cart for some time as it moved slowly down the dirt road. At a turn in the road, he finally lost sight of them.

Loren missed Tomi terribly in the weeks that followed. Determined not to show it in front of the others, he performed his duties. He especially wanted to be near her now, with their child growing inside her, but it was not to be. Her safety and that of the baby was paramount. He lived a life of priestly celibacy.

CHAPTER X—BATTLE!

In an all hands meeting, Loren announced that they would be curtailing their Coastwatching activities for the time being because of the heightened danger brought on by the increased Japanese presence. Time moved slowly as they performed their daily routines. In their last message, he informed their U.S. contact of the cessation of transmissions for the present. After a time, their contact responded that they were sending a man to work directly with them regarding their operational needs. They requested a suitable location to put their man ashore by submarine.

Loren plunged happily into organizing the covert landing. He generated a detailed message describing the location where the man could land and a time window. Late one evening, he went over the content with Dave. "I've given them a time frame to coincide with a moonless period. I've picked the cove where we originally came ashore on Mindanao as the best place to land. I've also told them that we would not be able to transmit again unless it was necessary to the mission."

"When do you want me to get on the road with this?"

"How about tomorrow morning?"

"I'll plan on starting then."

Dave set out on the road to transmit the message, far from their village. After five days, their U.S. contact replied that their man would land in the cove a week from the following Monday at 0200.

Ramon and Loren set off down the jungle trail to the cove two nights before their man's scheduled arrival. This allowed them plenty of time for the trip and they could keep out of sight during daylight hours. They arrived at the cove a little after sunset, with nothing more to do than to wait. The night was dark, with limited visibility. They stayed at the edge of the forest while Loren scanned the water with his binoculars, as the time grew near.

About twenty minutes before the appointed time, Loren saw a movement out near the entrance to the cove. As he watched, the dark shape of a submarine emerged from the water. A flurry of activity followed, as shadowy figures moved about the deck. He could hardly make them out. One of the men on deck dropped what appeared to be a black rubber dinghy into the water and a man jumped in after it. The dinghy and the man drew away from the sub and moved toward the shore, the man plying the water with a paddle.

"Let's go," said Loren as he stood up and moved toward the water's edge. With Ramon just behind him, they descended the last few yards. When they arrived at the beach, the submarine had disappeared and the man was almost to the shore. Ramon covered him from the rocks as Loren strode to meet the black clad figure in the dinghy.

"Lieutenant Middleton?"

"Right! Let's get off this beach as soon as possible." They carried the rubber dinghy up to the forest, where they had previously dug a large hole for it. While Ramon buried the dinghy, Loren shook hands with the newcomer in the dark.

"I'm Patrick McFadden. Office of Strategic Services."

"Loren Middleton. That's Ramon Vargas, headman of the village that we operate from." Ramon gave him a half wave as he labored.

"I'm anxious to see your radio setup. I understand that the Japs have become very frustrated trying to locate you."

Loren chuckled. "Really! We hadn't heard." A half-hour later they headed up the trail.

Loren spent the next few days briefing the O.S.S. man on their operations, while Dave and Tom proceeded to draft a defensive plan for the village. McFadden looked much different in the daylight.

Some three years older and a half head shorter than Loren, he had the look of his British forebearers with dark straight hair and gray eyes. He wore camouflage gear that he had brought in his small pack.

Loren showed him their transmission equipment and went over their procedures with him. McFadden was suitably impressed. As they worked together, Loren realized that the main reason for McFadden's visit was to encourage them to further effort, regardless of the increased Japanese presence.

"The information you have been sending us is fantastic! My boss back in Washington considers your operation a model intelligence facility. Many people would like to emulate exactly what you have done. Don't quit now!"

"If the Japs find us, there won't be any more model intelligence facility."

"I also want to talk to you about expanding your operations to adjacent islands."

"I'd thought of that. We would need someone to contact there and to work through."

"We can supply contacts. We have a man on the next island north of you, Leyte. He has been trying to establish an infrastructure like yours, but he has just started." They went on to discuss operations in detail, current and projected. McFadden ended up by asking him what his organization needed.

"We need a lot of things, new weapons, radio equipment, ammunition, supplies. What would really be great is some kind of compensation for these villagers who have been keeping us all this time."

"I'll pass your requests along to HQ. My boss, Bill Donovan, wants us to be able to support you however we can."

In two week's time, Ramon and Loren saw McFadden off to the waiting submarine in the darkness. They came and went like spirits in the night, with no one the wiser.

Loren was watching the sunset when he heard someone behind him. He turned to see Joanne standing closeby. "Hello, JoAnne."

"Hi, Loren. Did the O.S.S. man get off all right?"

"Yes, we put him on the submarine the night before last."

"Is he going to be some help to us here?"

"He says that he wants to. We'll have to see what he can do. How are you holding up, JoAnne?"

"All right, I guess."

"There's not much for you and Bev to do now."

"No. I guess that's a blessing. Bev has been spending a lot of time with Tom Kite recently, so she's been busy."

"Really. How about you?"

"I'm lonely."

Loren sighed audibly. "So am I."

"I thought you might be."

"There's nothing I can do about it, though."

"I thought that maybe we could see each other through this time."

"JoAnne, I can't. Tomi is carrying our child."

"I had heard that. I wondered if it was true."

"You see how it is."

"Yes. I've got to go back to my quarters. I'll talk to you later."

"Yes. Goodnight."

Loren reviewed the completed defensive plan with Dave and Tom. He liked what he heard, and they decided to adopt it. Loren briefed the plan to the naval contingent. "The plan has two parts, Cover Plan One and Two, which deals with attack from the road or from the jungle trails, respectively. In Cover Plan One, Buchman's fire team will cover the road, with the rest of us closer to the village with grenades and small arms if the intruders get through. Cover Plan Two calls for small screening teams fifty yards down the trails, with the main body ready to put crossfire on either of the trail heads. The Marine fire team would still cover the road to protect our rear.

"Also, Ramon has arranged for some outrigger boats to be available in the fishing village in case the Japs overrun us, and Leyte is closeby. With this scheme in place, I think that we are as ready as we can be." He left the floor open for further suggestions, but none were forthcoming.

Loren and Dave stood in the shade of a large tree in the blazing heat. "Dave, I've got a mission for you. I've just gotten off the radio with our stateside friends. They urgently need information about how far the Japanese have penetrated here on the East Coast of Mindanao and in what numbers. Pick your men and get ready to go tomorrow morning."

"Roger, Loren. We'll be ready."

Loren saw Dave and three of the sailors off on the mission to the south the next morning. With the increased Japanese presence, he knew that the danger was great, but they were at war and risks had to be run. He waved to them as they disappeared into the greenery at the edge of the village.

Time seemed to stand still as they awaited the return of the southern mission. In mid afternoon, Bev hailed Loren as he was walking back from the radio hut. "I need to go to the stream to bathe. Can you escort me?"

"Let me get the Thompson." He was back in a few minutes, the submachine gun slung over his shoulder. They took the trail back into the forest, saying little.

"I'll wait for you on this side of the hill. When you are finished, come on back."

"I will. Thank you, Loren." She disappeared around a curve in the trail. The stream, perhaps ten feet wide at the most, meandered down the length of their valley. A large pool at the trailhead facilitated bathing. Even at this time of year, the water was cold in the mountains and he didn't envy Bev her frigid plunge. He sat with his back against a tree trunk, cradling the Thompson. He was watching a bird in a tree when he heard her scream. Her voice sounded muffled, as if someone had a hand over her mouth. Loren leapt to his feet and ran down the trail in a crouch, the submachine gun at the ready.

He was to the edge of the greenery next to the stream when he saw them. Three Japanese soldiers had surrounded Bev. She was on her back on the ground with her coveralls down to her knees. One of the soldiers had a knee in her chest and was tearing the underwear from her body. A second soldier had unfastened his pants and had a sizable erection. A third was closeby, watching with a great deal of excitement.

Loren dropped to one knee and fired at an upward angle at the soldiers. The one who had Bev pinned to the ground rose bodily into the air and fell heavily beyond her. The one with an erection died with a look of surprise as the burst from the submachine gun caught him in the midsection. The third soldier turned to run as another burst hit him in the back. He sprawled forward and was still. Loren ran to Bev, watching the soldiers on the ground. They were down to stay. He knelt rapidly at her side and pulled her to a sitting position. Her mouth was agape and her eyes had a look of stark terror. She flung her arms fiercely around his shoulders and clung to him with surprising strength.

He held her and tried to comfort her. "You're safe, Bev. They're all dead. Let me help you with your coveralls." He helped her put her arms into the sleeves and pulled the zipper up the front. Then he heard cries and running footsteps from the village. In a moment, the others surrounded them.

"Jap patrol!" he shouted. "Fall out with full armament!" The navy men turned and sprinted toward the village. Loren followed, holding Bev close as they walked. She looked dazed. JoAnne met them as they entered the village.

"Help her, JoAnne!" The two women held one another for a brief moment and then Bev pulled away, looking frantically for Loren. He ran to find his ammunition and grenades.

They assembled in the center of the village. "OK, Cover Plan Two. Let's go." Two of the sailors went up each of the jungle trails while Buchman's fire team headed for the road. The rest of the armed contingent waited at the ready. Loren strode to the front of the group. Before he could speak, shots rang out down the southern trail.

"Deploy!" he called out and in seconds, the Navy men trained their guns in a crossfire on the mouth of the trail. The jungle around them was deathly quiet. Then they heard the sound of running feet. A Filipino farmer came into view. Loren saw, with a start, that the Filipino was the guide for Dave Blackmon's mission. "Hold your fire!" he ordered as the man ran into the village. Loren jumped up and went to him. He spoke to him quickly in Visayan. "Where are Lt. Blackmon and his men?"

"Dead, all dead!"

Loren felt as though someone had struck him a blow. "How?"

"I was late getting back to the point. The Japanese came up on them from the rear. I saw it all."

"What were those shots?"

"The navy men thought I was a Japanese."

70

Loren turned and walked slowly back to the line. He spoke so they all could hear. "I've just been informed that Lieutenant Blackmon and his men have been killed by the Japanese." A general murmuring erupted among the men. "As the Japs will be looking for their missing patrol very soon, we need to get to the boats in the fishing village immediately." He turned to Ramon. "Ramon, send a runner down the trail to tell them we're coming. Half of you pack your gear and get ready to go. Relieve the others when you finish. Fall back to the center of the village, now!" An hour later, they were in the midst of their preparations when they heard firing from the road. The Japs were coming for them! "Cover Plan One! Deploy to the road, on the double!"

The navy men dashed for the road on the dead run, their grenade bags banging against their ribs. They could still hear fire from Buchman's team as they dove for the deep drainage ditch alongside the road. With weapons loaded and ready at their side, they spread out ten feet apart and took grenades from their packs. Loren heard the sound of a laboring truck engine and then the truck came into view on the road.

"Get the Japs on the trucks!" he whispered hoarsely. "Don't let a single one get off into the jungle!" The truck lurched toward them. The troops riding in the bed were in obvious disarray. Loren was first to throw his grenade. It blew up under the vehicle, setting it on fire. He leveled his Thompson at the truck bed and pulled the trigger. He saw the Japanese troops go down before his fire. The troop truck, struck by additional grenades, careened off the road and turned on its side. Another grenade landed in the truck bed and exploded.

The second truck was upon them, traveling at high speed. Loren's next grenade went into its bed. Fire from down the line hit the truck's cab, shattering the windshield, while another grenade blew off the front wheel. The truck ground slowly to a stop, repeatedly rocked by the explosions of grenades thrown from the ditch. Nothing moved. Loren raked the truck bed of the second truck with machine gun fire. They heard cries of agony and then there was silence. A fire burned in the engine compartment, which triggered a large explosion as it reached the gasoline. A quick examination revealed no survivors. Just as well, Loren thought. They would have had to die anyway.

Then Buchman's fire team sprinted up to them on the road. Don looked at the carnage around them and then turned to Loren. "We got the other truck. Two casualties, fatal." Loren looked down the line in the drainage ditch. Ron Vanolli lay peacefully on his back, with a bullet hole in his forehead. One of Dave's crew lay just beyond him.

"We have to evacuate. Get your gear and we'll start down the trail to the fishing village." As they sprinted back, the sun was setting behind the mountains.

Loren saw Ramon with his weapon at the ready as they entered and went to him. "Ramon, we have to let Tomi know what has happened."

"I will go to her now."

"It will be very dangerous. They will be coming in force up that road!"

"I can avoid them." They stood looking at one another for a moment. Then they threw their arms around each other and hugged.

"Best of luck, Ramon."

"Go with God, Loren." He disappeared into the shadows. Loren turned and scanned the village. The villagers and the navy contingent had apparently departed. He did a cursory check for stragglers before heading down the trail. He had gone perhaps ten steps when he saw her. Bev was standing by the edge of the path in the moonlight.

"Bev, what are you doing here? We have to go now!"

"I waited for you."

"Come on, we have to go like the wind!" He took her hand and they plunged down the trail.

They moved rapidly all through the night. Loren, impressed by Bev's stamina, thought it was probably born of fear. At daybreak, they moved off the trail and eventually found a small clearing where they could rest. Loren lay back, exhausted, and Bev's head was between her knees.

"Where's JoAnne?"

"She went on ahead."

"You should have gone as well. Why did you wait for me?"

"Because I wanted to be with you." She said no more. Presently they both slept in the meadow grass.

They arrived at the fishing village after dark. Loren went to the house he knew and knocked. When the fisherman saw who he was, he hurriedly motioned both of them inside.

"The Japanese were here earlier. I need to get you out on the water as quickly as possible. Are there more coming?"

"I don't know."

The fisherman opened a trap in the floor and motioned them down the stairs. The dock under the house had an outrigger craft he called a banca moored there. He gave Loren and Bev some dried fish, which they devoured ravenously, and a large cup of water. Presently, another man joined them.

"Raoul will guide you to the next island. Go now, quickly!" With Raoul and Loren rowing, and Bev sitting amidships, the banca slipped smoothly out into the tidewater bay, and soon they were far out from land. They pointed the small craft in a northerly direction and Raoul set the sail. As the boat glided across the calm sea, Loren was glad to see no evidence of bad weather. Four and a half hours later, Raoul turned the boat toward the distant land. Large thunderstorms were forming behind them. They were on the beach an hour later.

CHAPTER XI—LEYTE

Local Filipinos met them at the water's edge and escorted them to a village close by. The village headman came to them a few minutes later. Loren and he had an extended conversation in Visayan, and then he left. Loren sat down on the tatami with his back to the wall. He stared straight ahead for some time and said nothing.

Bev came and sat by his side. She touched his hand. "It's not easy, is it?"

"What?"

"To be the leader, the one responsible."

He looked at her. "No, sometimes it's not. The Filipinos are going to guide you and me to the interior tomorrow. We'll use jungle trails. The village headman says that they have passed several of us along already." He paused. "Bev, less than half of those that were still alive when we left have arrived here so far. You are the first woman he has seen."

"Oh."

"There were storm clouds forming up behind us. If anyone else was out on the water, they might have had a real problem. I'm not sure how well those small boats handle in rough weather." Loren suddenly felt very tired. "We need to get some rest." He stretched out on the floor mat. Bev was close beside him.

"I'm here if you need me, Loren."

He looked into her eyes. "Why, Bev? I always thought you didn't like me."

"I owe you everything, Loren. If it were not for you, I would be a prisoner back on Bataan…or worse. If it were not for you, I would be dead at the hands of those Jap soldiers. If there's anything in the world that I can do to help you or comfort you, I will do it."

"You don't have to feel that way, Bev."

"I know, but I do." He held her hand as they drifted off to sleep.

Early the next morning, they plunged into the green jungle with their guide. Loren thanked the villagers profusely for the help they had given. He conversed in Visayan with the guide as they traveled down the narrow path. Then he dropped back to Bev.

"He says that it will take two days to get where we are going. We will sleep on the trail tonight. He also says that there is a place further along where we can bathe and clean up. I even brought some soap."

"Oh, that sounds wonderful!"

The heat and humidity were oppressive as they moved up the trail. Miniscule furry animals skittered across their path. About an hour after they had stopped for lunch, they came upon a beautiful waterfall cascading down over black lava rock formations to form a clear, deep pool. The guide spoke to Loren and then went off up the trail.

"He's going to siesta for an hour or so. We have plenty of time to do laundry and wash up. You go ahead. I'll be down on the trail when you're finished."

Bev looked into his eyes. "Loren, come with me."

"You'll want your privacy."

"Come with me. There is nothing of me that you haven't seen already." They walked hand in hand to the waterfall pool.

Loren pulled off his filthy uniform and plunged into the clear, bright water. Bev had slipped off her coveralls at the edge of the pool. She looked like a wood sprite, poised on the edge of the water. Then she leapt in as well. They spent the first few minutes soaping and rinsing their clothes and then stretched them out on a large boulder to dry in the sun. Then they took turns soaping all over. Bev did a heavenly job scrubbing his back, and he reciprocated. Then they lay down on another massive boulder to dry, naked in the sun. Bev caught him looking at her and she blushed a deep scarlet.

"You are truly beautiful, Bev."

"I've never done anything quite like this before, you know, but I like what I see too." They caught up with their guide a short time later and continued up the jungle trail.

"Hey, guys, it's the Skipper and Lieutenant Jones!"

A lot of backslapping and handshakes greeted them. Bev got some hearty hugs and some kisses that she hadn't expected.

Tom Kite was there, shaking Loren's hand. "It's great to see you, Skipper. We were starting to think that no one else was coming. What about the rest?"

"We were the only ones there when we came through. Just like you guys, they got us out of there as quickly as possible. I'm hoping that there were more behind us. What's the situation here?"

"From what I have been able to piece together, there is a real, full blown guerrilla presence here on Leyte. Not like our situation over on Mindanao. I haven't been able to get any details though. The Filipinos here speak very little English."

"I'll see what I can learn after we get settled." The headman of the rural village found accommodations for Bev and him. When he went into his assigned quarters, it struck him how meager were his possessions. Except for his .45 sidearm, he had no arms of any kind. He discarded the ancient Thompson when his ammunition ran out and had used all his grenades against the Japanese trucks. From what he had seen, the others were in the same situation.

Loren spent over an hour conversing in Visayan with the village headman. "Yes, there is a powerful Filipino guerrilla leader whose headquarters are up in the mountains," the chief told him. "He has many men and a settlement that even has a," he struggled with the word, "hospital."

"I must go see him and tell him we are here. We have fought the Japanese on Mindanao and killed many. I seek another man too, named Forrester. Have you heard of such a man?" McFadden had given him Forrester's name as a contact. The village headman, however, said that he did not know that name.

Loren called an all hands meeting after the midday meal and told them what he had learned from the village headman. "I will go up country tomorrow to meet their leader. I also have the name of a contact from McFadden's organization who supposedly is here on Leyte. I'll try to find him as well. I hope to get all of us gainfully employed against the Japs very soon."

Tom Kite took him aside after the meeting. "I don't think those that are left are very anxious to get back into the fray. They're a pretty tired, dispirited group."

"They can't stay here. The Japs would have them in their net before they knew what hit them. Why don't you see if you can drum up a little enthusiasm while I'm up country? I'm not sure how long that will be."

"I'll do my best."

Bev joined him as he walked through the village that afternoon. "Loren, I'm going with you."

"No, Bev. It's too dangerous."

"What am I going to do, just sit around here? At least there's a hospital where you're going. Besides, I want to be with you." Loren tried to reason with her, to no avail, and after a time, he reluctantly agreed. The two of them set out early the following morning, with a guide from the village. As they departed, Tom Kite gave him an inquiring look.

Four days and some hard trekking later, they arrived at guerrilla headquarters. They passed through a cordon of heavily armed Filipino troops. Loren talked to their commanding officer in Visayan, telling him who he was and who he was coming to see. The officer passed him through and provided a two-man armed escort. Upon their arrival, Loren went immediately to the guerrilla leader's field HQ. After answering several questions directed to him by another Filipino officer, he entered under escort into the presence of the commander. A small man with wispy gray hair and in field uniform sat at a desk in front of him.

"I am Lieutenant Middleton. I have come here from Mindanao."

"I am Colonel Kangleon. It is true then, you are Middleton? McFadden has told me much about you."

"Yes I am. McFadden? Is he here?"

"He is at the radio in the southern part of the island."

"I must see him as soon as possible."

"I will send him a message. Please sit down." An orderly brought some fresh brewed coffee. His host motioned him to partake. "Please go ahead. I drink only tea."

A long time had passed since Loren had the pleasure of drinking fresh coffee, and he enjoyed it thoroughly. He briefed the Colonel on the events that had brought him there, including the battle with the Japanese. "I still have some of my men who have made their way to Leyte. I believe Patrick McFadden will want them to be part of his mission. If not, we will fight in whatever way we can."

"Let us see what McFadden says when he arrives." Loren left a few moments later. Bev walked with him as they went to find quarters.

McFadden came in the next morning with a cadre of Filipinos. Loren came out to meet him and they shook hands in the dusty street. "My God, Loren, you're the last person I expected to see! What happened?"

"Come inside and I'll give you a rundown." Over two San Miguels, Loren told him of their discovery by the Japanese and the pitched battle that followed.

"But how did you get to Leyte?"

Loren described the small, outriggered bancas that had gotten them out. "When I left the village where we were staging, less than half of our people had shown up. I'm hoping that some more have arrived since I left. By the way, why are you here instead of back in the states? How did that happen?"

"Donovan sent me to relieve Forrester. I haven't had much better success in establishing a mission force than he had. I've got maybe a quarter of the number of men that I need and most of them are green."

"I hope we can be of some help, Pat."

"I'm certain you can. You understand that I'm responsible to Washington for this outfit."

"I realize that. It's certainly not a problem for me."

"You'll be in charge of the naval personnel. We need to train and integrate Filipinos into our covert operations."

"What about Colonel Kangleon? How does he fit into the command structure?"

"Our operations are independent of his. However, we support each other as the situation dictates. He's quite an old boy, you know. He must be over seventy. He spent twenty-seven years in the Philippine Army and he was the first native appointed a divisional commander by MacArthur. He surrendered to the Japs as part of the general capitulation and later escaped from a Jap prison camp, coming here to fight. Now he's trying to unite all of the guerrillas in this area so he can get some American aid."

"Sounds like quite an individual. By the way, what's our arms situation?"

"A small but complete arms suite."

"Automatic weapons?"

"Submachine guns, BARs, grenades and ammunition. We can arm our own people, but that's about it."

"That's a whole lot better than where we are now. All I have is a .45 and a couple of clips. Most of the others are in the same shape. What else do we need to discuss up front?" They went on to talk about various operational requirements as the day wore on.

In the next few days, Loren was able to relax for the first time in a long while. He had nothing specific to do as the Filipino guerrillas sought to move his men up to their headquarters. He had spent some time with McFadden planning future missions, but other than that, he was largely on his own. He explored the sizable village that had grown up around the guerrilla HQ, during the day. Perched on the highest ground in the area, with hundreds of thatched huts around them, were the HQ buildings, screened from view by large green trees. As many as three thousand people were living there, according to the estimates he had heard. Surrounded by jungle, the heavy greenery gave them some cover from the occasional Japanese overflights. From the air, Loren thought, they must look like any of the villages in the surrounding countryside.

Bev had been looking at their medical facility, which was more like a dressing station, as she described it, than a hospital. He thought about her and her newly found attraction to him. She was lovely and this was war. Tomorrow, he might not return from one of his missions. Living for the moment seemed the thing to do.

From where they were, he could see the craggy mountains of Mindanao, far to the south. Out there somewhere was Tomi...and their child. Many months had passed and he or she would have been born by now. He wondered if he would ever be able to find her again, once the war was over. They were half way through 1943 and the end was nowhere in sight. By now, her father had a price on his head, if he was alive. The Japanese dealt harshly with family members of a guerrilla. A strong possibility existed that none of them would survive this war.

He found that several attractive Filipino girls had made a special point of making his acquaintance. Flattered by the attention, he enjoyed talking with them. They apparently knew that he had a Filipino girl when he was on Mindanao. Bev had been watching all of this and she was unhappy.

She came to his quarters late one evening and they sat together on the palm mat in front of the charcoal brazier. She was still wearing the old faded khaki coveralls that she had back on Bataan. Loren sought her hand.

Bev looked down at the palm fronds of the mat. "I watched you with that young, pretty Filipino girl today, that Mila. Is she going to be the one?"

"The one?"

"I know that as a man you need physical gratification."

"With Tomi it was a lot more than that. When she left the village, she was carrying our child. I hope that wherever she is, she is safe and well."

"Loren, I didn't know. I'm sorry." She was quiet for awhile. Then she turned to look into his eyes. "I love you very much, you know. I want to be everything to you in every way, but I'm not sure that I can be. You told me at the pool that you were attracted to me physically, but I may not be able to be what you want. I've never done anything, so I don't know."

He remembered her, lying next to him on the rock at the falls, and how beautiful she was. "I would like there to be us, Bev." He held her closely as he touched her dark, glossy hair. She turned her face toward him and they kissed, for the first time. He held her closely, in his arms.

In the next few days, they discovered one another. Their first time together was warm and loving and a short while later, they experienced the joy of giving pleasure, each to the other. Loren was scrupulously careful that she not get pregnant. He loved tracing the contours of her body with his hand and seeing her naked caused a spasm of desire in the pit of his stomach. They were blissfully happy and content.

CHAPTER XII—THE CLANDESTINE WARRIORS

The Mindanao survivors came trooping down the main street and Loren was there to greet them. "Tom, good to see you."

"Good to see you too, Loren. It's good to be here."

"Looks like a couple of more showed up."

"Yeah, Mike Hanson from your crew and one more from ours."

"That's great. Did you hear of anyone else that might be on their way?"

"Hanson said that he thought two more members of Dave's crew were coming right behind them, but when we left we hadn't seen or heard of them."

"Anything on JoAnne?"

"Nothing."

Loren called a meeting for the navy people that afternoon. He reintroduced Pat McFadden and then talked to them regarding their role in the Leyte operations. At the conclusion, he summarized their situation. "We'll be dividing our time between actual covert missions and training the Filipinos to participate. We're going to be damned busy! Now get some rest and we'll start assigning tasks tomorrow."

The next few weeks were as busy as he had predicted, with rigorous training exercises interspersed with treks into the jungle to gather intelligence. Loren started to train the new Coastwatchers immediately. The training went much more easily because he did not have to work through an interpreter.

Weapons and ammunition were in short supply, so they performed training exercises by "snapping in," which meant performing the firing motions with no ammunition. Loren drilled the new men repeatedly in formations and movement through enemy territory, plus gathering and dissemination of data. Soon, he began integrating selected candidates into one of the experienced teams for actual missions.

Recruiting picked up with the inclusion of the local Coastwatchers on the guerrilla payroll. The guerrillas went so far as to set up a provisional government, which in turn began to issue currency. Everyone on the island accepted the paper pesos at their face value.

Throughout their preparations, he and Bev were together whenever they could get free. During these times, they talked about things like where they had come from and how they had grown up, and the things that were important to each of them. Loren found that Bev was an intelligent, well-educated woman, now that she had opened up at last. For the first time in a long while, Loren thought about the future. They became as close as two people could be.

Sometimes they talked about what had happened on Mindanao. "Loren, when all of this is over, what are you going to do about Tomi and your child?"

"I'm going to try and find them. That is, if I survive. After that, I don't know."

"Don't talk like that Loren, about surviving. We're going to make it through, I know we are!"

The Coastwatcher's roster was pretty well full, and Loren's training efforts started to taper off. One day, McFadden announced that he was going to lead a mission to determine Japanese troop dispositions to the north.

"You're going to lead a mission, Pat?"

"Why, does that surprise you?"

"Well, I guess I've always thought of you as an administrator, an expediter, rather than someone who actually ran missions." Pat told him at some length of his experiences in France in 1942. Loren listened in respectful silence.

McFadden received streams of requests for information from Washington via Southwest Pacific HQ in San Francisco. Their overall mission was developing into something quite different from what they had done on Mindanao. Southwest Pacific HQ, or Souwespac, now became very interested in ship movements in their area. This in turn required more or less permanent manning of stations in remote areas, with less powerful radios transmitting data to the master radio at the Guerrilla HQ. Loren initiated a rotating assignment schedule to these remote places.

Souwespac's area of particular interest was the San Bernardino Strait above Samar, but they also requested the establishment of stations around the islands of Samar and Leyte. Their appetite for intelligence data in these areas seemed insatiable.

Pat McFadden and Loren discussed the rapidly changing developments. "What do you think all of this means, Pat?"

"I can't say for sure, but it looks like they're planning some operations in this area. To what extent I couldn't say."

"Wouldn't it be something if they were going to land somewhere around here."

"That it would, that it would."

"Pat, I'll be heading out tomorrow to establish the radio station on Samar." Samar was northeast of Leyte and overlooking the San Bernardino Straits. "This station will be the furthest one out. We're going to have to cross the water from Leyte to the island."

"I know. I assume you'll be heading for the fishing village up on the northeast corner of the island."

"Right. The local population is supposed to be in sympathy with the guerrilla movement. We hope to get them to row us across to Samar."

"Sounds like a good plan. Best of luck."

Loren thought that, at best, this was going to be a difficult undertaking, with heavy concentrations of Japanese between them and their objective. The army had supplied them with two technicians to help in the initial installation of the radio equipment. The radios, salvaged mostly from the old Philippine communication system run by the post office, had been exceedingly hard to find. The one that they planned to install on Samar was the last in their inventory. Spares were nonexistent.

Loren was in the center of the formation as they carried their heavy burdens on the jungle trails to the north shore. Two men were at the point out in front in case they should encounter Japanese troops. A fire team was close behind to protect the precious cargo. The tangled greenery was all around them, teeming with life. The shrill cries of the tropical birds interrupted the ever-present hum of the insects. Loren and the others were soaked to the skin as tropical rain showers beat down on them. Ponchos were not an option in the intense heat and humidity.

They approached the village cautiously, in combat formation. The villagers saw them and came forward, greeting them warmly. After they had introduced themselves, Loren negotiated with the chief for transportation over the water to Samar. "With all of our equipment, we will need several bancas." They were the type of dual-outrigger boat the Navy men used to escape to Leyte.

"We have many bancas here in the village, one that is close to forty feet long and over three feet wide," the chief replied.

"Do you have any that are motor driven?"

"No, the bancas all have a native rigged triangular sail. Some of the larger ones have two masts."

In just a few minutes, Loren reached an agreement with the chief and the installation team moved out from shore with three of the larger bancas. In the black of night, the fishermen rowed them out to open water and then set sail. As they glided across the smooth water, Loren hoped the favorable wind would hold until they passed the routes of the Japanese patrol launches and landed on Samar.

The men made landfall about two hours before sunrise. Loren addressed the company, speaking in a whisper. "Unload the radio equipment and make up loads for the march up country. We need to get off this beach as soon as we can." He spoke to the villagers who had accompanied them across the water. "We will be here at this time five days from now. It's important that we get back to Leyte before sunrise, so be here on time. We will see you then."

Loren and the installation team moved into the trees and followed a jungle trail in the general direction of their proposed radio site. They had been in luck so far, he thought. During the next day and a half, the team climbed to the central ridge and then down the other side. The afternoon of the second day, as they left the dense forest, they discovered an almost perfect vantage point to observe the San Bernardino Strait, the main waterway from the South China Sea to the waters off the eastern islands.

Loren addressed the Filipino work party. "All right, we're not going to find any better place than this. Get started on the leanto back in the trees. We'll set up the small feeder radio and the portable generator in it."

"Yes, sir."

The army technicians cut the wire for the antenna to a length that was a function of their transmission frequency, according to the tables in the radio manual. Loren watched them hang the antenna wire between two trees and then run a lead down to the equipment in the leanto. Then the technicians grounded the radio and hooked it up to the four storage batteries.

The team had brought a twelve-volt generator as well, to keep a charge on the storage batteries. Loren had to chuckle as he examined the jury rig of two six-volt generators working together via a belt and pulley. They had been very fortunate in finding these generators, recently liberated from the Bureau of Constabulary, the BCs.

The BCs were Filipino policemen who worked for the Japanese in maintaining internal security. Loren knew that the local Filipinos tolerated these people only because they were much less of a problem than having Japanese troops in the area. Some of his people had broken into a BC compound in the dead of night a week or so ago and removed several generators and fan belts from the BC vehicles.

Loren had put out pickets for the duration of this initial installation, and now he organized a relief.

"You men stay awake out there. There are a lot of Japs on this island."

"How long are we going to be here, sir?"

"Until the army gets that radio going. Each watch will be four hours, starting now."

"Yes, sir."

The army technicians bent over the radio, trying to make it work, while the others in the party got some rest after their long cross-country trek. Loren longed to stretch out in the grass and sleep, but there were too many things to do. On the third day, after many fruitless tries, the army men were, at last, able to reach the Guerrilla HQ on Leyte. While they were waiting, Loren saw to the unloading and storing of the supplies for the two-man crew that was to man the station for the next month.

Loren's team packed up and started back on the fourth day for their rendezvous with the men from the fishing village. The going was much easier, with most of their burden left at the radio station, and they arrived at the bay where they had initially landed in the afternoon of the fifth day. They rested on the edge of the dense forest and waited for the night, keeping an eye out for Japs. As the sun set over the water, Loren was jubilant about how well the installation had gone.

Loren was increasingly restive as the hours went by, with no sign of the villagers and their boats. He was just about to give up and start thinking of alternatives when the villagers in their bancas arrived. "Where have you been?" he said in a loud whisper. "You're nearly two hours late!"

"We had trouble locating the pickup point in the night."

"Let's get loaded and out on the water. Move it!"

He and his men, with their equipment, were in the bancas and under way in twenty minutes. He had just breathed a sigh of relief when the wind slackened.

Exasperated, Loren called out. "Now, what?"

"We've lost headway, sir. We are going to have to break out the oars and scull the boats across the water."

Exhausted, they arrived at the village long after sunrise. Miraculously, it appeared that no one had seen them crossing. Loren barked out orders. "Get your field packs organized for the trip back. You've got ten minutes!" At last, they set out down the main street of the village for the trailhead. The morning sun was well above the horizon.

With Loren out in front, they were halfway down the main street when the crackle of rifle and machine gun fire sent them diving in the dust for whatever cover they could find. Loren rolled behind a tree trunk and looked for the source of the bullets whining past him. The sound of automatic weapons reverberated throughout the village. A Jap patrol was firing at them from a hut at the head of the street!

"You, you and you come with me!" Loren barked out in Visayan. He and three young Filipinos raced down the alley that paralleled the main street. They flung themselves down at the point where the alley swung out to join the street. They were thirty yards away from the nipa hut where the firing had come from. He looked at the three Filipinos who had come with him. They looked scared. He wished that he had some grenades, but there were none.

Loren looked again directly at the three young men. "Cover me!" He ran toward the hut in a crouch, with his Thompson at the ready. Another bullet whined by his head. He raked the front of the hut with his Thompson and heard a scream. A low wall to his right offered some cover and he ran for it. More bullets zipped by him, but then a fusillade of rifle shots struck the front of the hut. His cover men were on the job. He saw movement in the doorway and fired from a crouch. A Japanese soldier pitched forward down the ladder and lay still at its base. Now there was firing from behind the hut as some of the others worked their way up.

When the Japanese returned the fire, Loren dashed across the street and dove under the nipa hut, landing on top of a scrawny white chicken. With feathers flying, the hen raised an infernal racket. Bullets thumped in the dirt beside him as he rolled on his back and squeezed the trigger of his machine gun. The magazine was empty in seconds. Through the chinks in the floorboards, he saw uniformed bodies, unmoving. The house was quiet.

Loren saw Hanson with a Springfield just beyond the back door and waved him over. "Cover me, I'm going in."

He drew his .45 automatic and raced up the stairs. The sailor was just behind him. They burst through the door, looking for any sign of life in the darkened room. Loren caught a movement in the corner of his eye, whirled and fired four shots into the soldier against the wall. The man's breath expired as he slumped to the floor.

"Check them all, Hanson. If they're alive, finish them off!" Hanson took a couple of minutes to ascertain that the members of the patrol were indeed dead. Later, the team gathered outside the house.

One of the Filipinos died in the ambush, but they reported no wounded.

Loren asked one of the villagers to get the village headman. When he arrived, they talked for a moment. "If you get rid of these bodies and everyone keeps quiet about this, no one will ever know what happened to these Japs. Bury them way back in the jungle or weigh them down and dump them in deep water." The headman said he understood.

Loren found, after the adrenaline receded, that he had a slight wound in his right shoulder. After some first aid, he was ready for the trek to the south. They reached Guerrilla HQ in good time, and Loren dismissed the team with a "well done." The experience had been a sobering one.

After this mission, he found that his stock with the Filipinos had risen even higher. His first hint that something was up was when Pat McFadden came in and gave him a hearty slap on the back. "Well, my boy, you are really famous now."

"What do you mean, Pat?"

"Some of the Filipinos that were on this last mission with you told Colonel Kangleon about the fight in the fishing village. He transmitted a full report of the action to Souwespac. The rumor is that you are going to get a Philippine decoration for valor in the field." McFadden was beaming like a proud parent.

"I don't understand what all the fuss is about. We just tangled with a Jap patrol."

"That's not what I have heard. I hear you really did a job on those Japs."

"There were several of us."

"No false modesty now, my boy. We've had our share of the bitter. Let's enjoy some of the sweet stuff too." They left it at that.

The tense, dangerous missions Loren ran had become a large part of his life. When he had time between operations, he had as his constant companion the pretty, enigmatic Miss Beverly Jones, Lieutenant, U.S. Navy Nurse Corps. When they were together, she was surprisingly passionate, considering that she had been so cold and aloof toward him for so long. He was not quite sure how this transformation had taken place, but he was grateful for it as they clung together in the night.

One morning, as they were getting ready for the day, Bev came to him and put her arms around his neck. "I'm staying here from now on, Loren. It doesn't make sense for me to run back to my quarters every morning."

"Are you sure you want to do that, Bev? Everyone will know."

"Everyone knows already. Yes, I am sure." And so, they lived together openly. They were inseparable and every day was finer than the last.

Loren noted in passing that several of the naval contingent, including Ensign Tom Kite, had set up quarters with the very attractive local girls he noticed when he first arrived at the guerrilla HQ. Tom's girlfriend was exceptionally beautiful and he was the picture of a happy man. Loren had some long thoughts with regard to the combat readiness of the men under these conditions. All of this had come about through the many social activities of the village.

One of the things that he had noticed early on was that the Filipinos there were great party people. Their entertainment featured a native drink called tuba, drawn from the palm tree. By itself, it tasted very bad, but the Filipinos effectively disguised it by mixing it with combinations of sweet-tasting ingredients. Tuba was not overly strong alcoholwise, but enough of it would serve the purpose. The first time Loren and Bev tried this concoction, they had lingering headaches all the next day.

At the parties they attended, there were few luxuries in the way of food, but on a given evening, a Filipino sideboard would contain beautiful fruit salads with mangoes, pineapple, papayas and shredded coconut.

The Filipinos held numerous dances, with girls on one side of room, boys on the other. The girls of course required chaperones but, as it will, love found a way. As it was on Mindanao, the family of a Filipino girl felt singularly honored if an American chose her.

Loren told Bev about Mestizos. "Mestizos, or mixed-race children, have a high value here in the Philippines. When the Spanish ruled here, whites were at the top of the social scale. That's still true, even now. If there is any white blood at all, a person is white by

Philippine standards. Because of this, Americans who are fighting against the Japanese are not only greatly admired, they are considered desirable mates as well."

She smiled at him. "What about American women?"

"Forget it. I'm not planning on sharing you with anyone."

When Loren returned from his last patrol, Bev had examined his wounded shoulder. "This needs to be tended to. Come with me to the hospital."

"Bev, it's just a bullet crease."

"If something like that gets infected you can lose that arm."

"All right, let's go."

In the small hospital, she applied sulfa powder directly to the wound and put on a clean dressing. "There. That's better. We'll change that again tomorrow."

Loren reached for her and took her in his arms. "Thank you for watching out for me."

Recently, Bev had started working closely with the local doctors and dentists, recruited for the hospital. Scouring the surrounding area for medical instruments, the guerrillas' plan was to bring them all together in one place for the common good, she told him. "There are pitifully few instruments, so they're easy to carry from place to place. In that sense, we are a mobile hospital unit."

Loren chuckled. "There's not much business anyway, is there?"

"Well, just local emergencies and the occasional wounded soldier."

"Pat says that the guerrillas don't initiate large-scale operations against the Japanese because they're so woefully underequipped."

Bev smiled a wry smile. "Anyway, small as it is, the hospital's ready."

CHAPTER XIII—THE GUERRILLA OFFENSIVE

Pat McFadden briefed Loren on Colonel Kangleon's success in uniting the many small local guerrilla bands that formed on Leyte after the Japanese came. "The Colonel also undertook the task of establishing ties with a large guerrilla group operating in central and southern Mindanao, commanded by the American Colonel, Wendell Fertig," Pat went on. "Souwespac recognized his efforts and agreed to run supplies and ordnance to the guerrillas by submarine."

"When will the first sub be here?"

"Very soon. One thing that's of interest is that they can take personnel out with them under military orders."

Loren thought of Bev. When he saw Pat later that day, he brought it up. "Pat, about that sub that is bringing the supplies…"

"Yes?"

"What about Bev? Could they take her out?"

"I'll check and see. I've got a meeting with the Colonel later this afternoon. Let's see what he says. Does she want to go?"

"I haven't talked to her about it, Pat. I'll do it tonight."

He broached the subject with her as they lay on their pallet. The discussion was short and to the point. "Loren, no. My place is with you, wherever you are. I won't leave you, no matter what."

"But Bev, there is extreme danger here. The Japs may overrun us tomorrow."

"No."

The next day, he talked to Pat again. "She doesn't want to go."

"That's sort of what I thought. Colonel Kangleon said that, if she wanted to stay, they needed her expertise at the hospital. I sure can't order her out and neither can you."

"I know. I guess things will just have to stay the way they are."

The submarine arrived at a cove some miles away. A small army of Filipinos unloaded the cargo and then carried it to the guerrilla camp. Loren was part of the contingent that had gone down the trail to the shore. They watched the sub surface in the black of night and immediately become a beehive of activity. It contained a cornucopia of supplies they had only been able to dream of. Ordnance, ammunition, uniforms and food were just some of the items coming out of the hold. The cargo included bazookas, .50 caliber machine guns on tripod mounts, 20mm cannons, Thompson submachine guns, carbines, grenades, and even soap, razors and razor blades. Basic medical supplies like Atabrine for malaria were included as well. They would be a ragtag outfit no longer.

Loren found his way to the submarine's wardroom where he met her Captain and his Exec. They were both amazed at finding American naval personnel out in the wilds of the Philippines. While they had some coffee, Loren entertained them with the story of how it had all come about.

"Will you be coming out with us?" the Captain asked.

"No, sir. I'm going to be fighting my war here until you guys come back for good."

"Well, we should be making this run pretty regularly from now on. We hope to see you again." They shook hands and wished each other the best of luck, and Loren went ashore for the long uphill hike to HQ.

Loren replaced his ragged navy uniform with a new summer weight one that the sub had brought in. He kept his battered naval officer's cap. He showed Bev the new razor and the supply of blades he had gotten from the submarine.

"Oh, how wonderful! I haven't seen your face in so long!" Loren had had no razor blades for some time and he had been keeping his beard reasonably trim with an old pair of scissors that Bev had brought home from the hospital. His first shave was traumatic, as he cut back his heavy beard. Bev passed her hand over his smooth cheek afterwards. "That's much, much better." She was especially loving that night.

Colonel Kangleon's army, now fully equipped for taking the offensive, started getting ready. The next few days saw a marked increase in training exercises. Loren knew that before the submarine had come, the local population largely supported the army. Their guns and cartridges, as well as their food came from the town people. An occasional ambush netted them some Japanese supplies, but that was risky because of the chance of retaliation against the poorly equipped guerrilla army.

About seven hundred guerrillas were in the Colonel's army and, before the arrival of the first sub, only about half had rifles. The troops that Loren encountered when he first came to the guerrilla headquarters shared their rifles with the next watch when it came on. He remembered with a smile, his first impression of the guerrillas, armed to the teeth.

The army's most important accomplishment, as far as Loren could see, was a homemade telegraph that stretched one hundred forty kilometers to the southern part of the island. They had used Coke bottles for insulators. All of this now changed as the Filipinos made ready to take on the Japanese.

Loren watched all of the activity and wondered what was coming. When they were alone for a few minutes, he asked Pat about it. "It looks like the Colonel is making plans, Pat. Do you know anything about it?"

"Not to go beyond this room, but yes, the Colonel is planning a large-scale offensive in February."

"If he stirs the Japs up, that might not be good for us."

"You had better talk to him."

Loren voiced his concerns to Colonel Kangleon. "If the Japs come up here looking for guerrillas, they might clobber our intelligence gathering missions instead."

"No, Lieutenant Middleton. We will strike small garrisons that you have so thoughtfully pinpointed for us that are away from our home base. We will force the Japanese to send out patrols to find where we are. We will be waiting for them."

The plan sounded good to Loren. "What you have to look out for is if the Japanese make large scale landings on Leyte to cope with your operation like they did on Mindanao. They eventually discovered our base because there were so many of them."

"If it comes to that, Lieutenant, there will be a whole lot less of them than when they started."

Loren thought about pressing the point regarding their initial agreement with Colonel Kangleon to provide soldiers to defend the radios they had sited, but thought better of it. Despite the agreement, the promised soldiers had never materialized.

With McFadden's consent, Loren addressed the Coastwatcher personnel, which had grown close to platoon strength, in Visayan. "You are all aware of the coming offensive that Colonel Kangleon is organizing. When a firm date is set, it will be our function to provide security for the master radio station. We'll apprise the outlying stations of the offensive by radio and tell them to be alert for possible retaliatory action. The cordon of troops that is normally protecting the HQ will be thinned out drastically to support the offensive, so, if the Japs come our way, we must be ready to fight. We will post pickets at some distance from the station and run reliefs every four hours. There will be no more missions until after the offensive. We will spend the time developing defensive earthworks around the station. We'll post a plan for this, with a schedule, tomorrow. In the meantime, see that your weapons are clean, and draw some ammunition."

In negotiations with Colonel Kangleon, Loren obtained two tripod-mounted .50 caliber machine guns, which he sited so that they would have interlocking fields of fire in the direction from which the Japanese would most likely attack. Well-armed and ready for battle, they waited.

H Hour came and Loren's men watched the guerrilla army march off into the green jungle. In the nerve wracking days that followed, the people at the radio station had no way of knowing how the engagement was going. Once, they heard small arms fire in the distance, but then they heard no more. In their defensive positions, the tension crackled as they continued their vigil.

Finally, on day five, part of the guerrilla force returned with several wounded on stretchers. Loren sought out Major Castillejos, one of the Colonel's officers. "Manuel, how is the offense going?"

"The troops report that the actions are going well and that Japanese casualties are heavy."

"That's good news. I'm glad."

Bev went to the hospital and Loren saw very little of her for awhile. Two days later, more of the guerrilla army returned with stretcher bound wounded.

In the next three days, the rest of the guerrilla army returned in company size groups. The hospital filled to overflowing with the wounded. Bev was working long, hard hours. "The morale of the returning soldiers is really high," she told him. "By all reports, the action has been a success."

"That's terrific! It will be interesting to see what happens next."

After being cut to pieces in their encounters with the guerrillas, the Japanese stopped sending out patrols and they were observed retiring to the seacoast. Loren thought they would be back in force.

Reports started to reach him of large-scale Japanese reinforcements landing on the island. Loren sent out multiple missions to try to determine their strength and intentions. He talked to Pat about it. "The flat country around the towns on Leyte doesn't offer much cover. This has really hampered our efforts. It appears that the Japanese are going to hold the coastal areas in strength and leave the interior to the guerrillas, at least for the time being."

Pat looked at him and smiled. "That's good for us. By the way, there's another submarine due to come in very soon. With more supplies to sustain the Colonel's operation."

Loren shook his head. "It's going to be more difficult to offload the sub undetected, because of the Japanese reinforcements."

"Colonel Kangleon has decided to mass a large number of troops around the submarine rendezvous and deal with any Japanese patrols that might stumble upon our operation. If the Japs show up, it's going to be lively. I want you to go with the unloading detail as liaison again, to smooth over any communication problems that might arise."

"Wouldn't miss it, Pat."

As before, the submarine surfaced just outside the cove and then hove to close to shore. The Filipino workers started the unloading process immediately. When Loren went aboard, he found two Navy men, an officer and a first class, in combat gear getting ready to go on shore. The sub exec introduced them. "Gentlemen, this is Lieutenant Loren Middleton, USN. Lieutenant Middleton, this is Lieutenant Bill Falk and Aerologist's Mate 1st Class Norm Williams. The orders are for you to assist them in establishing a meteorology station on Leyte."

Bill Falk looked like an academic, Loren thought. He could picture him, smoking a pipe. Norm Williams was young and very outgoing. The new Navy men had a considerable amount of gear to unload, including rasonde and pilot balloon instrumentation.

Loren briefed them on the operation. "Your first task is going to be a long, hard climb up into the mountains. The Filipinos will transport your equipment to our camp. We could also have Japs on our neck any time while we're here on the coast, so stay on your toes. Other than that, it's a nice tropical night for it. Welcome to the Philippines."

Later in the night, as they climbed away from the cove, Loren talked with Williams about what was happening stateside. "You wouldn't believe how short the skirts are getting, sir. It's supposed to conserve cloth or something. Bob Hope got cut off the air the other night for talking about powdering four cheeks. And the girls are wearing leg makeup instead of silk stockings."

"That, I'd like to see," Loren replied with a broad grin.

Besides the meteorology gear, the sub brought a large suite of medical equipment for the hospital. Bev had been telling Loren how limited their treatment options were, but now all this would change. The submarine had also brought new navy radios to replace the antiquated, jury-rigged equipment out in the field. Before Loren left, the submarine captain told him that they would be coming to resupply them regularly now.

Bill Falk had just finished getting his meteorology station in place and working, when McFadden received a message from Souwespac directing them to chart the minefields off Samar and radio the information back.

Loren and Pat talked about it. "What do you think of this, Pat?"

"It looks like invasion of the islands is not far off. Are you ready to set out for Samar?"

"We will be by tomorrow morning."

Loren led the mission to the remote radio station on the far side of Samar. They were taking a new radio for installation at the observation point, so the personnel roster was pretty much the same as their initial installation effort, except that Tom Kite would accompany them as well.

"You'll be leading the mission back while I stay on to chart the minefields, Tom. I hope that this trip is a smoother one."

"Piece of cake, Skipper."

Loren planned to stay on at the remote site for five days to do the charting, using his army compass with the sighting vanes over the compass face to track Japanese ship movements through the mined area. Using this device, which they had called a pelorus at the Academy, he could measure and compute distance and time, bearing, course and speed of a vessel passing through the minefields, and thus determine where the clear channels were. The relief observation crew he was bringing along would continue to report whatever ships would pass.

Again, it took the army technicians who had accompanied them two days to get the new radio up and working. The new radios looked like they might be as cantankerous as the old.

Loren said goodbye to Ensign Kite and the rest of the team as they headed back down the trail. "Best of luck, Tom. I'll be seeing you in a few days. There are lots of Jap patrols around, so be careful."

"That I will, Skipper. See you when you get back." Loren watched them go single file down the jungle path.

Loren had kept one of the best Filipino scouts with him to help him with the readings from the pelorus. As he read off the numbers, Carlos Delgado noted them on a pad. Swarthy, with dark, piercing eyes, Delgado had been one of Loren's best pupils and was the first of the trainees to go on an actual mission. After four days of watching and tracking, the routes through the minefields started to repeat, and Loren surmised that they had what they needed. He coded a message containing his numbers describing the minefields and relayed it via the new navy radio to the master set at the HQ. Loren and Carlos made ready for their return through the jungle to the rendezvous with the fishermen. They had finished a full day early, so they rested and enjoyed their sojourn. Loren attempted to converse with Carlos, but he had little to say.

The night of the fifth day, the two men disappeared down the jungle trail into the blackness. They moved rapidly over the uneven terrain and soon reached the crest of the island. They had been traveling about an hour downward toward the water, when Loren heard a metallic click.

"Jap patrol!" he whispered hoarsely. "Off the trail!" They dove into the underbrush. Within seconds, Loren saw Japanese soldiers coming in single file toward their hiding place. The soldiers trudged silently past them, with one man trailing the column and acting as a rear guard. Suddenly, the rear guard stopped directly in front of Carlos and thrust a bayonet toward where he was hiding. Carlos rose slowly from his hiding place with his hands above his head. Loren attacked the soldier from the rear, locking his forearm across the man's throat. He felt the bone snap in the man's neck and his body go limp. Loren picked up the lifeless soldier and threw him into dense greenery by the side of the trail.

"Let's go!" he whispered to Carlos. They ran silently down the jungle trail.

Loren and Carlos arrived back at HQ in the evening. After greeting Bev, Loren showered and cleaned up before falling into a deep sleep. The next morning he went to see McFadden to file his report.

When he arrived, Pat gave him a searching look. "Well, you're famous again."

"What do you mean, Pat?"

"Your scout told the other Filipinos about your encounter with the Jap patrol. He says you killed one of the Jap soldiers with your bare hands."

"I had to take him out, or he would have alerted the rest of the patrol."

"Colonel Kangleon is beside himself with praise for you. You are probably going to get another medal."

"There's no call to make such a big deal of it." Loren proceeded to give his detailed report. When he returned to his quarters, it was apparent that Bev had heard of the encounter as well. Her demeanor toward him was subdued, and she regarded him mostly in wide-eyed silence.

CHAPTER XIV—INVASION!

They had not seen or heard a Japanese aircraft for a long time, so the drone of engines in the distance surprised them. As he ran out of the HQ building, Loren's first thought was that it was a bombing raid. A few seconds later, he found the formations on the horizon. The aircraft were coming directly toward them. He was about to sound the alarm when he saw, through his field glasses, the white stars in a blue circle on the leading aircraft. They were American planes! The roar of engines grew steadily louder as they came closer. When they passed overhead, the roar was deafening. No one there had ever seen that many aircraft in the air at one time. They came over in huge formations, rank after rank. Bev ran to Loren's side and clung to his arm as they looked up in wonder.

They came again and again, every hour all through the day. Everyone watched the massive formations until they disappeared in the distance. The aircraft, with their dark blue upper fuselage and white on the underside, were obviously carrier based. Loren had not seen some of the new types before. The following day, they came again, wave after wave of planes on missions of destruction.

"I wouldn't like to be where they're going," Loren observed, "not on the receiving end." The others agreed.

Bev watched with them. "What does it mean?" she asked.

Loren shaded his eyes. "It looks like something big is coming."

101

Then they came for a third day, but Loren could still not take his eyes from them. The awesome power they represented fascinated him and those around him. Then, as suddenly as it had begun, it was over. They all had a sense of anticipation for the future. The time was mid September.

Loren was not sure what it was that had awakened him in the early morning hours. He raised up on one elbow and listened. Then he heard it, the far away rumble of explosions that were almost continuous.

Bev raised a tousled head from her pillow. "What is it, Loren?"

"Listen." Then she heard it as well.

"What do you think it is?"

"The Americans have come, Bev." They dressed quickly and hurried to the hill overlooking the village. They climbed rapidly to the top and then stood in awe of what was before them. The entire horizon was alight with guns flashing in the night. After they had watched for a few minutes, they went down to the master radio to see if the operators had picked up any official announcements. As they came in the door, a voice on the main speaker was declaring the invasion of the Philippines on that 23rd day of October, 1944.

Loren and the rest of the naval personnel had gathered at the radio station to listen to the reports that described the changing scene. Not only had the American troops come ashore, but an immense naval battle was taking place as well. Except for the crews manning remote observation sites, the immediate need for intelligence data had dwindled to nothing. The American Army knew, without question, where the Japanese Army was now. Loren checked incoming reports that indicated much movement of Japanese naval units in the San Bernardino Strait. The fleet received this information, forwarded on their send frequency. That must be a hell of a show, he thought to himself as he listened to the rumble of the big guns in the distance.

They had watched the flashes of artillery fire and heard the thunderous reports move slowly toward them from their vantage point at the radio transmitter. Then the battle seemed to move away from them to either side.

Loren addressed the naval personnel. "This may be the time to try to make contact with our forces out there. I'm going to head east and have a look."

He went to his quarters to get ready for the trip. Hearing someone behind him, he turned to see Bev in the doorway. "Loren?"

He looked into her eyes. "Come with me, Bev."

"Yes."

They quickly prepared light marching packs and headed down the jungle trail to the lower hills. In the next two days, from various vantage points, they saw the columns of Japanese troops on the roads in the valleys below, headed towards the west. On the third day, there was nothing. The hills and valleys around them were eerily quiet.

Loren scanned the area below them with his glasses. Satisfied, he put them back in their case. "Let's go down and have a look." Bev and he moved cautiously down the jungle trail and in an hour, they were on the floor of the valley. From the edge of the trees, Loren swept the surrounding area with his field glasses. He saw no movement. The whole fertile valley looked as though it was uninhabited.

They walked out into the meadow and down to the narrow road. Loren led as they walked down the deserted dirt track. He halted as he saw movement in the trees at the bottom of the hill. Loren and Bev flattened themselves on the grass of the verge as he scanned the area below. Then a group of men in combat uniforms came out of the trees and moved toward the road. Loren saw, with a lump in his throat, that they were not the Japanese. He stood up and slung his Thompson over his shoulder. Bev was by his side. They walked slowly down the hill, hand in hand.

The army major stood in front of them. "You are Lieutenant Loren Middleton, USN? I'm supposed to be looking out for you and members of your group. Is it true that you've been here in the Philippines since 1941?"

"Lieutenant Jones and I have been here from the beginning."

"That's amazing! I've got the motor pool commandeering a vehicle and driver to send you back to the rear. There are a lot of people who want to talk to you."

In thirty minutes, they were in the back seat of a Buick command car and on their way. Bev nestled close and put her head on his shoulder. They found that they were both very tired and, after awhile, they slept.

Bev entered the cruiser's wardroom looking fresh and beautiful. Loren was having coffee with the ship's Exec. She flashed them a radiant smile.

"Well, that was an experience! I almost had a sailor walk in on me while I was taking a shower. The marine guard stopped him just in time." Both Loren and the Exec chuckled at this. Bev wore no makeup and, with her fresh glowing complexion, she looked like a girl of sixteen. Loren watched her as she spoke. She looked as though the cares of the world had been lifted from her shoulders. He felt the same way. They were guests for lunch and American food never tasted so good.

That afternoon, a ship's launch took them to a waiting PBM Mariner that would fly them to Hawaii. Bev was close beside him as they flew eastward over the vast ocean. Loren turned to look at her. "That's a good looking uniform the Navy dug up for you. A little large, maybe."

"They did all right by you as well. I don't think we would pass an inspection though."

"There's plenty of time for things like that now."

Bev smiled and put her arm through his. "Yes, I know. Isn't it wonderful?"

"Yes it is. By the way, the Exec on the cruiser told me that we were in for an extensive debrief when we get to Hawaii. I asked him what it was all about and he said that it's all very hush hush."

"Really? They want to talk to me too?"

"That's what he said. I suspect that they won't keep you long, though. We'll see when we get there." Many hours later, they set down on the beautiful blue water just opposite Ford Island in Pearl Harbor.

CHAPTER XV—THE LONG ROAD HOME

The Navy gave Loren and Bev two days for the QM to issue them new uniforms and for them to get generally shipshape. Bev went to a hair salon for the first time in many, many months and Loren submitted to the rigors of a regulation haircut.

On the third day, they met with the people who were to debrief them. They scheduled in-depth interviews with Bev, much to Loren's surprise, as she really had no direct part in their covert operations. When he reported at 0800, squared away in his new summer uniform, the duty officer directed him to a meeting room. In the room, a group of people, mostly in civilian clothes, sat around a large table. As they went around the table for introductions, Loren learned that most of those present were from the Office of Strategic Services, the O.S.S. The Navy Captain who was presiding brought the group to order.

"You may be surprised to learn, Lieutenant, that you have been working for some of these men for many months." He went on to tell him about the surprise and amazement that greeted the first messages from Mindanao that Loren's group had sent. "When we learned that you and your people were not currently part of any existing intelligence agency, the O.S.S. moved quickly to have you assigned to their organization. The Navy complied as requested.

"General MacArthur has a guerrilla warfare unit and a comprehensive intelligence system, called the Allied Intelligence Bureau, under his command," the captain continued. "The Philippines were in his theater of operations and he effectively blocked O.S.S. operations there because he feared interference from Washington. The presence of your group and the transmission of intelligence data under the auspices of the O.S.S. caused a huge political flap. Neither side was willing to back down while you were in place in the Philippines, but the situation has changed now that you are finally out from behind the lines. We want to go over your operations with you so we can understand how everything worked."

The debrief team showed interest in every detail of the day-to-day operations in the Philippines, both on Mindanao and later on Leyte, because the missions were quite different.

In the afternoon of the fourth day, the captain in charge of the debrief summarized. "Now as I understand it, Lieutenant Middleton, you devised a mission plan based on gathering what information you thought would be valuable to the intelligence community and devised procedures to gather this information and transmit it to us."

"It was a team effort, sir. Several members of the team gave us input in areas where they had expertise. We were also generally familiar with what the Coastwatchers did."

"You also devised training for the Philippine nationals to participate in intelligence gathering missions. This effort was expedited by your fluency in the native dialects."

"Yes, sir."

"How did you learn these dialects?"

"From the local populace, sir."

"You just picked it up as you went along?"

"I had some very special help."

"And you also led intelligence gathering missions."

"Yes, sir."

"I think that will be enough for today, Lieutenant Middleton." The captain was looking at him with a look verging on respect. "I have another meeting with these gentlemen now. We'll reconvene at 0800 tomorrow."

"Yes, sir." Loren rose and left the room.

That night at dinner, he talked with Bev about his experiences so far. "I think I told them everything they wanted. I don't know whether they believed me or not."

"When they talked to me, they wanted to know every detail of how the medical side was performed. Number and kind of doctors, what instruments we had, what medicines, what drugs. Also, they asked me about what it was like to be a woman working in a behind-the-lines situation."

"What did you tell them?" Loren asked with a grin.

"I tried to be noncommittal." They both laughed about this.

Loren's debrief finished late Friday morning. The captain had one last thing to say before they adjourned. "Lieutenant Middleton, we want you to join the Office of Strategic Services in Washington on special assignment. We are going to promote you to Lieutenant Commander and make you head of our Philippine operations."

Overwhelmed, Loren didn't know what to say. Finally, he managed to stammer a reply. "Thank you, sir." Then the captain closed the meeting.

Bev and he received orders to report for a flight to San Francisco the following day, for thirty days survival leave. Apparently, the navy considered them in the same category as if the enemy had sunk their ship. In a small ceremony that afternoon, the Admiral commanding the Naval District conferred the Navy Cross for gallantry on Loren along with another half stripe. Bev was at his side.

At dinner that evening, all the sunniness seemed to have gone from her. Loren wondered, but decided he would wait until she told him, in her own time, what was wrong.

They were having a last cup of coffee after dessert when she told him. "Loren, the Navy is talking about having me come back here for duty when our leave is over. And you are going to Washington." She had tears in her eyes as she looked away.

Loren looked at Bev across the table. He thought for a moment before he spoke. "Well, that's an easy problem to solve."

"But how?"

He took her hands in his. "Beverly Ann Jones, will you marry me?"

She looked into his eyes. "Oh, Loren," she said quietly, "of course I will."

He just had time to go into Honolulu to find a jeweler before their PB2Y Coronado took off for the mainland. As they settled back into their seats for the long flight, Bev held her hand up to the light to see the sparkle from her blue-white diamond engagement ring. The sunniness was back.

The big Coronado touched down on San Francisco Bay and, in a few minutes, Loren and Bev prepared to deplane at Treasure Island. It felt strange, Loren thought, to be back in his own country after all this time. The crew had piped some popular music back to the passenger cabin during their long flight in and he hadn't recognized any of it.

Loren talked with the crew chief as they flew towards their destination. "Yeah, Commander, things have changed a whole lot since you've been away. The government rations just about everything and almost everybody is in the service or working in a war plant. Even my brother-in-law has a war job and he hasn't had a job in years!"

"It looks like the Navy is a lot larger than it was."

"Oh, yeah, sir. There is ten times the amount of carriers here in the Pacific than there was in the entire navy before the war, maybe more. The carriers are the way to go, now. They just use battleships to shoot up the islands before the Marines go in. The little ships, there's no counting them."

Loren and Bev checked in at T.I. and received their quarters assignments. They learned that Navy installations in the San Francisco Bay area traditionally do not change to summer weight uniforms. After a quick trip to the cleaners to get their winter uniforms in order, they emerged in navy blue dress for their dinner date at the Mark Hopkins. They had a cocktail at the O Club and then caught a cab into the bustling city. Loren discovered that Bev looked smashing in her blues. They were full of one another as they dined. Afterward, they went for a drink at the Top of the Mark. Low clouds spoiled the view, but they had eyes only for each other, so it didn't matter. One of the features of the bar was a real reclining nude, mirrored up from where she lay, so that the patrons could observe as they enjoyed their drinks.

Loren thought that was a great idea. "You know, you might do really well in a job like that, Bev."

"Why don't we go to Fisherman's Wharf or something, Loren?"

Later in the evening, she was telling him about Oregon as he sat and watched her. He wondered what the odds were that he would marry a missionary's daughter who had never known any man but him. He knew that she loved him deeply, and he could not help loving her in return. He remembered the day at the lava rock pool and the first time they had known one another in the wilds of the Philippine jungle.

Then Bev was asking him about travel arrangements to Portland, interrupting his reverie. "I'll pick up the tickets tomorrow. We have military priority so there should be no problem. I'm hoping we'll be flying the day after." They sat looking into each other's eyes as he held her hands in his.

Loren and Bev arrived at Portland Airport, aboard a crowded United Airlines DC-3. Her parents had invited him to stay at their home and were waiting at the passenger gate when the couple arrived. Bev rushed into her mother's arms. Both were crying. The Reverend Jones pumped Loren's hand. "It's good to meet you, at last, Loren." He beamed up at him. "How was your trip?"

Loren grinned at his prospective father-in-law. "This last leg was better than the first two."

"Let's get the luggage and we'll be on our way."

At first, Beverly's parents didn't quite know how to take Loren, the man who had spent all that time in the jungle with their daughter. With the help of his dress blue Lieutenant Commander's uniform and the prominently displayed Navy Cross ribbon, he was able to win them over. Her parents showed him her high school and college yearbooks, and the traditional baby pictures. They were very coy about the picture of Bev at six months without her diaper.

They spent most of their leave preparing for the wedding, with no privacy at all. Bev introduced him to the rest of her family and her friends, who were slightly in awe of him. They had all read the local newspaper's censored account of their experiences in the Philippines.

Then the day came and they took their vows in the church where Bev was baptized, her father presiding. Loren was the only member of his family present because, with wartime travel restrictions, it was impossible to go anywhere without a military priority. Then they were on their way to the Oregon Coast in an old Ford.

Beverly's parents had managed to hoard some gasoline so that they could make it that far. Gas was rationed and an A card gave them only three gallons a week. They spent the few days left of their leave in a cabin that overlooked the ocean, watching the storms roll in. The weather was terrible, but they didn't mind.

Bev's family saw them off on their transcontinental train ride. Through the magic of their priority military orders, they got a sleeping compartment for the journey. The happiness peculiar to newlyweds was upon them. They sat hand in hand watching the mountains and then the prairies roll by their window. They interrupted their sightseeing at regular intervals with intense lovemaking on the clean, crisp sheets.

Loren was lying back on the pillow of the berth with Bev in his arms. Kansas was passing by their window. He ran his hand along her waist to her hip. "Hi, you."

"Hello."

"I wonder if other people have traveled coast to coast naked like we are."

"Probably. I guess I won't write Mother about it, though."

"You don't think she'll understand?"

"She might," Bev said with a smile. Then they were embracing once more.

The only time that they left their compartment was to go to the crowded dining car, jammed with uniforms. A day later, they changed trains in Chicago, boarding another express liner to Washington, D.C.

They arrived at Washington's Union Station late in the afternoon. His family was waiting for them at the gate and they made a big fuss over Beverly. Loren hugged his mother and father as they stood on the platform. His Father's voice was husky. "Welcome home, Son." His mother had tears in her eyes.

"Thank you. I'm glad to be home at last."

He organized their bags and had a red cap deliver them to the street exit. Their luggage had grown considerably, thanks to Beverly's extensive shopping trips in San Francisco and Portland. After Loren loaded their luggage into the car, his mother and father drove them out to Ft. Meyer in the Virginia countryside.

Loren presented his orders and received their housing assignment to transient quarters, and the family dropped them off. His mother talked to him before they left. "Now, Loren, you have to promise to bring Beverly out to the house this weekend. There'll be family and friends there who want to see the two of you."

"Yes, Mom, we'll be glad to come." They waved goodbye as the family drove away. Loren and Bev were the only Navy people on the large, populous army base.

CHAPTER XVI—O.S.S.

Because of his position in the O.S.S., Loren rated a car from the motor pool. He used it to join the crowded commuter traffic into Washington and his office. He was officially on detached duty to the Army on special assignment. He could not discuss his highly classified assignment with anyone except his fellow officers and Bev. The O.S.S. made a decision to read wives into the program some time before, so that an inadvertent slip would not occur within the walls of someone's home. Loren was happy with this. His day-to-day life was a whole lot easier if he could discuss his job and its issues with Beverly, if he needed to.

He was not surprised to find that Patrick McFadden was to be his immediate boss. They had a happy reunion and spent the better part of a morning swapping stories on their extraction from the Philippines.

Loren was telling him about their abrupt departure. "They just picked us up and sent us immediately to Hawaii for debrief in a matter of hours. We never did know what became of the rest of the unit."

Pat told him what had happened. "I stayed on in the Philippines for several days to do an orderly shutdown of the group, but some of the other naval people were spirited away in a hurry as well. The army shipped Tom Kite out the day they made contact with us at the radio station."

"Where's Tom now?"

112

"He's still enjoying his survivor's leave, but he is scheduled to join us sometime next week. Which reminds me, I hear congratulations are in order for you and Bev."

"Thank you, I'll pass that along."

"After you get a little time to settle in, we'll have to have a get together of some kind. Say hello to Bev for me."

"I will."

The following Monday, Lieutenant Junior Grade Tom Kite came through the door of his office. "Whatta you say, Skipper! I understand you're a married man and everything!"

"You got it!" Loren walked around his desk to shake hands. "It's good to see you, Tom!" They spent the next hour catching up on all that had happened since the Philippines.

Tom leaned back in his chair and looked at Loren. "So you and Bev are married! I'm really looking forward to seeing her again."

"I think Pat is planning a party in the next couple of days. If not, you'll have to come over for dinner anyway."

"You're on, Skipper."

As they settled into their life in their sparsely furnished quarters at Ft. Meyer, Bev and Loren found that the social life of a member of the O.S.S. was very structured. Because of the level of secrecy their jobs entailed, they tended to socialize with O.S.S. families to the exclusion of others. With both spouses read into the program, there was not a chance of passing information to an uncleared person.

As promised, the McFaddens held a soiree, with all of the Far East contingent invited. Tom Kite was there with a striking blonde. He bussed Bev very convincingly in his joy to see her again. Loren remembered Tom's interest in her in the early days on Mindanao.

Tom drew Loren aside later in the evening. "Have you heard anything about the rest of our people that were on Mindanao?"

"I've asked several times, but no one appears to know anything."

Tom paused. "Have you heard anything from the Filipinos we knew? I gave Felice, you know my friend on Leyte, my address here in the states, but I haven't heard a thing. I know that you and Tomi…and Ramon were very close."

"They seem to have disappeared off the face of the earth. My inquiries have turned up nothing."

"I guess we'll have to wait and hope for the best." The two men returned to the party.

On their way home, Loren told Bev about his conversation with Tom. "I was going to ask if you had heard anything," she replied. "It must be terrible for you, knowing that you have a child out there somewhere in the Philippines."

"I don't know that for sure, either. I don't know if anyone survived. I'm going to keep looking."

"I'm sorry, Loren."

For their first Christmas together, Loren and Beverly went to visit Loren's family on Christmas Eve, but Bev was far from her own people. "You know, I've gotten used to having a family again after all of that time in the Philippines. I really miss them."

"I know, Bev. Maybe the war will be over by next Christmas and we can go out to Oregon for the holidays."

"I sure hope so."

The newlyweds thought about having a small open house on the afternoon of Christmas Day, but their neighbors came and went so quickly in the transient housing that they really didn't know anyone. They had a quiet Christmas dinner, with lots of leftover turkey.

With the holidays, and Loren and Bev getting settled in, Loren really didn't get started in his new job as the Head of the Philippine Islands Operations Department until after the first of the year. He found himself once again dropped into the middle of a political hotbed, with the O.S.S. fighting for its postwar life against a plethora of bureaucratic foes. This ongoing struggle had intensified in the fall of 1944, with General Donovan pursuing his goal of a postwar central intelligence agency that reported directly to the president. The general, known for his charisma, purportedly had the ear of the president, according to McFadden.

McFadden called Loren into his office on the Monday after New Year's. "I've got an assignment for you, to get you started on your new job. I'd like you to draft a comprehensive report on the current situation in the Philippines, along with general recommendations regarding future operations there and in similar overseas situations. I also want a training guide for O.S.S. personnel scheduled for insertion into hostile country in the Far East, based on the methods you developed in the Philippines.

"Also, this intelligence will not be useful unless it gets disseminated in a timely manner, so I'm going to lay an ambitious schedule on you to complete this work."

They spent the next hour going over the details of the assignment. The tasking was a tall order for Loren to complete in the short period allotted to him. They planned to distribute the report to the State Department, to demonstrate the expertise that was available in their current organization.

"What about people, Pat? If we are going to recommend ongoing operations, we are going to have to train a cadre of Philippines based agents for them."

"Right now, our staffing levels are frozen, but I'll see what personnel might be available for that kind of an assignment in other areas."

In the next few weeks, Loren worked long days and weekends on the material that his boss requested. He had a secretary, a homey young lady who was a whiz at typing and proofreading, to help him put his documents in shape. He noticed her watching him one day as they worked. "Yes?"

"Do you mind if I say something?"

"Shoot."

"This is the most incredible story I have ever heard. All that time behind the enemy lines! You are a brave man."

"We did what we had to do."

Loren made time to find out about the organizational struggles to create a longterm intelligence plan. He found that two groups were strongly against the formation of a centralized intelligence function, the military intelligence organizations and the State Department.

Incongruously, the State Department found reports generated by the O.S.S. to be very useful to them, especially those from the Research and Analysis Branch. O.S.S. Counter Intelligence also sent many reports to State that they found useful. Despite that, there were those who thought the O.S.S. was encroaching on traditional prerogatives of the State Department. The diplomats were particularly suspicious of the organization and saw it as a potential rival.

After an internal review, the O.S.S. released Loren's final report on the Philippines under the auspices of the Research and Analysis Branch. McFadden talked to him about it at the end of the review. "It's good that we got R & A to release this. They have been the most successful of the O.S.S. organizations in interfacing with other government agencies. They're composed of academicians, mostly from the Ivy League, and their job is to sort and cull raw data from the field and come up with estimates of an enemy's capabilities and intentions. They also drew conclusions on things like civilian and military morale, and diplomatic intrigue."

"They didn't have much analysis to do on this."

"I know, but this will make sure that your report will be widely read. R & A's greatest claim to fame is that they have developed a structured method of performing intelligence research. Their organization has become increasingly involved in the military side of things as the war has gone along. They are a highly respected organization in the Capital."

"I hope you're right, Pat."

Loren's report, well received at the State Department, contained recommendations for further O.S.S. activities in the field, such as liaison with active guerrilla groups and the newly restored Philippine Government. Also included was a proposal to monitor Japanese efforts to reinforce their military by Coastwatcher personnel, strategically placed.

McFadden talked to him about it. "If these recommendations are approved, you would be the prime candidate to implement them. However, General MacArthur's command, which as you know has its own intelligence capability, is against any O.S.S. presence in the islands."

"Sounds like politics, Pat."

"Too true. There is also the question of whether there is a need for further clandestine activity in the Philippines, because the campaign there is drawing down."

"What can we do to get them off the dime?"

"Just wait, my boy, just wait. Upper management is working it."

The battle for Leyte was essentially over by the first of the year, with only some mopping up to do. The invasion of Luzon took place in January, eventually forcing the Japanese Army back into the mountains and forests around Baguio. They were little better than a guerrilla band now, with few supplies, less ammunition, and with no hope of resupply.

McFadden told him that, with General Donovan having personal access to the President, something might come of his recommendations yet. On a cool April day, Loren was passing McFadden's office when Pat motioned him to come in. His expression was somber. "I've just had a call. Roosevelt is dead. He died down at Warm Springs, Georgia."

"My God!" He reflected for a moment. "I thought he was indestructible, that he'd be there forever. How will that affect us?"

"I wish I knew, Loren."

The political infighting continued, until it was too late to do anything effective in the Philippines. In the same time frame, The O.S.S. proposed a special operation to infiltrate the Kurile Islands and obtain direct intelligence on Japanese defenses. Loren's selection for this effort was a matter of course.

Pat talked to him about mission requirements. "You're going to need some special training before you take this on, Loren. There's a lot of new hardware that's been developed for shows like this that you need to get familiar with."

"Let's get it underway, Pat. There's not much time before we have to go."

"Have you ever had formal training in hand-to-hand combat?"

"No."

"I'll schedule that for you as well. Your participation in this will really help the organization. It will show them what we can do."

The team was ready to go when orders came to cancel. They gave no reason as to why. The cancellation was a real letdown for Loren and all of the team members.

With the stressful job situation he was experiencing, Loren found increasing pleasure in going home at the end of the day to Beverly and their government furnished home at Ft. Meyer. She had been very busy of late, going into Washington for private sales of furniture and accessories. They both knew that it would be some time before they saw new furniture and appliances in the stores, so Bev was trying to make intelligent choices for their permanent home, wherever it might be.

"I've got it all stored downtown at a warehouse," she told him. "I almost have enough to furnish a house, when we get one."

"That's great! One day soon, this will all be over and we'll be looking to get our own place." In the meantime, they enjoyed their blandly furnished quarters and just being together.

A little more than three weeks after the President's death, General Eisenhower declared Victory in Europe. The spirits were high in Loren's department, but they held no celebrations yet, like the ones in Times Square in New York City. They all knew that they still had a very large task awaiting them, the subjugation of the Empire of Japan. The casualty lists from Okinawa were very long and everyone knew that the assault on the main islands would be costly.

Loren and Bev were going to an O.S.S. party again that night. All the parties appeared to be either organization oriented or project oriented over more than one organization. Tonight it was one of the latter, celebrating a milestone reached by the O.S.S.—China organization. There were a large number of attendees. During the course of the evening, someone from the office introduced them to Bob and Cara Lee. Bob was one of the R & A people that Loren had been reading about lately, a Ph.D. mathematician with a reputation for being very bright. His wife, Cara Lee, was very attractive and a top-notch golfer.

Bev was excited when she talked to Cara Lee. "I was on the Lady's Golf Team at the University of Oregon. I've been wanting to get back into golf for a long time!"

"Why don't we try to set something up later in the week?"

"I'd love to play some golf again, but I have to tell you that I haven't been able to play for a long time. I'm very much out of practice."

Bob had been listening to their conversation. "Middleton. You wouldn't be the people that were in the Philippines during the Japanese occupation?"

"Yes, we are," said Loren.

"We've been reading about you in the Post. I also believe that I have your preliminary report about the Philippine situation on my desk! No wonder you are out of practice, golf wise!" They spent a few minutes talking about the censored version of their experiences that had appeared in the Washington Post.

Bob was a shortish, very personable individual. His dark hair and horn rim glasses made him appear owllike at times. Cara Lee was a fair-skinned beauty, voluptuous and very social. Her stylishly cut brown hair framed her oval face and her deep brown eyes shown as she talked. Loren thought that they were a most unusual couple.

Bob was speaking. "Look, we need to get a golf foursome together. I'm a real hacker, but Cara Lee is terrific!"

"I've played very little golf," Loren replied. "Bev has been after me for some time to go out and play a round. If you can put up with my indifferent play, I'd like to give it a try."

"Done! I'll set something up at the club for Saturday."

The next few weeks saw the two couples playing eighteen holes every Saturday. Beverly was rusty and, in their first two outings, didn't do well. Suddenly, on the third weekend, she played on outstanding round, beating Cara Lee by a stroke. The happiness showed in her face as she left the eighteenth green for the clubhouse. Loren gave her a large kiss. "That was a hell of a round of golf, young lady."

Bob echoed the sentiment. "Outstanding, Bev."

Cara Lee smiled at her. "I'm going to have to get to work on my game. You're too good."

Bev blushed as she smiled. "Thank all of you. Now I have to see if I can do this consistently."

Loren was a different story. The other three had to spend a lot of time waiting for him, as he attempted to get himself out of difficult lies. On one occasion, he hit a ninety-degree slice that landed on the adjoining fairway, with other players hitting toward him. With the same single-mindedness he used to solve difficult problems, he addressed the game of golf.

They played some of their matches at the Ft. Meyer golf course, which was less crowded than the courses closer to the city. Loren met the golf pro there and talked to him about lessons.

"What areas of your game do you want some help on?" the pro asked.

"All areas, from driving to putting. I've got the worst slice in captivity."

"Let's go out and hit a few and I'll see what I can do for you."

Soon, the ninety-degree slice was a thing of the past, and Loren started hitting big, booming drives that landed far beyond the tee shots of the others. Then the rest of his game started to improve as well. Yet, he still felt that something was wrong with his approach to golf, because he came off the course more tense and stressed than when he started. "I wish I could approach the game like Bob," he told Bev. "He has a lot of athletic ability, but he's content to play at the level he's playing at now."

"He does have a relaxed approach to golf. His interests seemed to be more in the social aspects of the game."

"Nothing wrong with that. I just wish I could relax a little when I'm playing."

As time went on, Loren noticed that Bev and Cara Lee were becoming increasingly competitive and soon they were scheduling mid-week matches with some of the other wives, while Bob and Loren were at work.

The two couples decided to have dinner out Friday evening. Cara Lee suggested one of the nicer restaurants in the downtown area, and they agreed to meet for cocktails at Bob and Cara Lee's before. They came in the door as Bob was shaking the martinis. Cara Lee had on a smashing short, black cocktail dress that showed her off to great advantage. Beverly was elegant in a navy blue party dress. Bob and Loren sat at the kitchen table imbibing martinis, while the women did last minute touches and adjustments. Bob was discussing a football pool card that he was going to fill out. "Honey, do we have a pencil here somewhere? I need to fill out these football pool selections."

"Right there on the bar."

"Where on the bar?" Cara Lee came into the room and over to where they were sitting. She turned and reached across the bar, lifting her leg as she did. Loren had a clear view, up to her silken panties. He swallowed hard, and Bob turned to smile at his nonplused look.

"There," she said, handing him the pencil and then leaving the room. A few minutes later, they were on their way in Bob's big '42 Oldsmobile.

Their dinner was elegant and Cara Lee paid special attention to Loren, conversing with him all through the meal, almost like they were on a date together.

"We've got to show you this great place we discovered," Bob was telling them. "It's the best club of its kind that we've found."

"Sounds good. Lead on." They drove for perhaps a mile, and then pulled into a parking lot on L Street. The Exotica Club was across the street and down a half block. They entered the darkened club and sat at a table close to what appeared to be a stage. They ordered a round of drinks, and Loren was just settling back in his chair when, with cool jazz sounds, the curtain opened. On the stage was one of the most beautiful women he had ever seen. Dressed for evening at the start, she removed various items of clothing as she danced. At the close of the number, only sequined pasties and a g-string kept her from being completely nude. Loren glanced at Bev, but she seemed caught up in the spirit of the moment. After an hour and more exotic females, Bob suggested that they head home, as it was getting late. They were in animated conversation as they walked back to the car. No one said anything about what they had just seen.

Cara Lee put her arm through his. "Loren, come sit in back with me so we can talk." Loren smiled and opened the door for her. She was talking about the restaurant that they had been to earlier. She sat very close to him. The short black cocktail dress that she wore had crept well up her thighs, revealing lovely curvaceous legs. Loren turned toward her as they talked. She looked into his eyes and then reached out to place her hand on his hair. She brushed his lips with a kiss. "There. I've wanted to do that for a long time."

Loren was amazed. Then she was in his arms and he was touching her, everywhere. He felt her tongue in his mouth as he caressed her under the enticing black dress.

She pulled back slightly and looked at him. Her brown eyes were shining and she had the slightest smile playing at the corner of her full lips. Her beauty overwhelmed him and his excitement was apparent.

He moved to kiss her again but she held back. "I thought the four of us might be one happy family," she said, looking into his eyes.

Loren stopped short and then glanced at Bev, who was in animated conversation with Bob in front. "Not in a million years," he spoke quietly. "Bev is a puritan."

Cara Lee pushed her hair back. "That's unfortunate. I would have enjoyed us. You never can tell about women though. Sometimes, the straight-laced ones will surprise you. If anything changes, call me." She kissed him again, lightly, and straightened her dress.

CHAPTER XVII—THE END OF THE OLD

The O.S.S. began preparations for a clandestine mission into Korea, which was very similar to the one proposed for the Kurile Islands. Selected again to be on the infiltration team, Loren immediately set about getting ready. The mission, tentatively scheduled for the third week in August, moved into an advanced state of preparation. As they worked, Loren began to hear vague rumors of a powerful secret weapon, but no confirmation was forthcoming.

The jumpoff date for the new mission grew closer and Loren became increasingly restless. He had been playing in a handball league at the base for some time and now approached each match with a savage intensity that others remarked on. If he had a particularly competitive match, he sought to get his opponent out to play again during the week. During the Philippine Island political wrangle, he had felt chained to his desk, but all of that was now past.

He talked to Beverly about it that evening. "Bev, I'm going to be out of the country for a few days."

"Oh? Where?"

"I'm scheduled to attend a Theater Commander's briefing in the South Pacific. I can't tell you where."

"How long will you be?"

"It's sort of open ended. I should be back in a couple of weeks, though."

"I'll miss you, darling. Please be careful out there." Beverly was aware of the special training he had undergone recently and Loren knew that she was watching his day-to-day activities. He wondered if she had an inkling of what was coming.

At a reception to celebrate the promotion of one of their colleagues, they ran into Bob and Cara Lee. Bev told them about the trip. "Loren is going to be out of the country for a couple of weeks. He can't tell us where, other than the South Pacific."

Bob gave her a serious look. "In that case, you'll have to come over for dinner while he's out there consorting with those native girls. You wouldn't believe what goes on during these junkets."

Loren was laughing. "All right, Bob. Let's not give away any military secrets."

As they talked, Loren watched Cara Lee. Ever since the time in the back seat of the Olds, he had fantasized about her. He watched her changing facial expressions as she talked in her animated way. In each plane of her face, there was beauty. Loren noticed the concerned look that she gave him when they talked of his overseas trip. She was not frivolous now. She seemed to want to say something, but apparently thought better of it. He looked at her and wondered what she was thinking.

Now, O.S.S. activity suddenly accelerated on the Asian mainland. Loren heard rumors about missions in northern China, and especially Indochina. Of course, there was no official confirmation because of the system of compartmented clearances in use. Only those actually participating in an activity had a clearance and a need to know officially about it. Nevertheless, the running of clandestine missions throughout Southeast Asia seemed to be common knowledge at O.S.S. HQ.

As the day grew closer for him to leave, Loren was increasingly aware that what he was about to embark on was really a side show, that and all the other O.S.S. activities on the mainland of Asia. On the islands of Japan was where the struggle was looming. This would make everything that went before it pale by comparison.

He knew that the Japanese nation, man, woman and child, was waiting for them on Honshu, Kyushu, Hokkaido and the many smaller islands. They had little use for advanced, sophisticated weaponry in their preparations. They believed that strength of mind and spirit and their veneration of the emperor would lead them to victory over the enemy, the barbarian who threatened their shores.

Loren heard that three Marine divisions would invade the home islands in the fall. The estimated battle casualties to defeat the Japanese were a million men. Although he was not aware of it at the time, what awaited the Japanese instead was Trinity.

A government task force exploded the first of the triumvirate in the southwest desert at Alamogordo, New Mexico, in mid July, though only a tiny portion of the Washington populace knew of it. Then, in early August, Colonel Paul Tibbets lifted the Enola Gay off an airstrip on Tinian and, with two other B-29s, flew off to his destiny. The news of the total destruction of the city of Hiroshima blared from the radios and extras, with large, black headlines describing the event, were on the street.

Loren, in his office at O.S.S. Headquarters, was astounded at the news. He quickly called Bev. The phone rang twice before she answered. "Bev, the most amazing thing has happened! They have dropped a single bomb on Japan that has destroyed an entire city! Turn on the radio and listen."

"I will. What does it mean, Loren?"

"It means that the war will be over soon, at least that's what I think."

"I hope you're right, darling. I hope that all the killing and bloodshed will finally stop."

The whole city of Washington was at a fever pitch. Then, three days later, the Army Air Force obliterated the city of Nagasaki with the same awesome weapon, harnessing the energy of the sun. They had crushed their implacable enemy into submission. Amazingly, the long, brutal war was over!

Loren walked down to Pat's office. Pat rose as he entered and they solemnly shook hands. "Well, Pat, it seems that we are out of things to do."

"Only for a little while, Loren." Then some revelers burst in and the moment was lost.

The O.S.S. offices were in a frenzy of celebration. Long-hoarded bottles of bonded bourbon and scotch suddenly appeared and then disappeared as the party went on.

The formality of V-J Day was a short time later, a week before their scheduled mission into Japanese occupied Korea. With the termination of hostilities, O.S.S. units went into Manchuria to free American POWs. Among the first to be liberated was General Jonathan Wainwright, the last American Commanding General in the Philippines during the dark days of 1942. These operatives, who had been so active in the latter stages of the war, would be the nucleus of an American postwar intelligence network on the Asian continent, if the O.S.S. survived the bureaucratic warfare in Washington. Loren hoped they would.

The summer showers inundated the Washington area that weekend, washing out their regular weekly golf game with Bob and Cara Lee. Being housebound and watching the rain come down from the large window in their living room was a nice change. Loren and Beverly were relaxing on the living room couch. Only a few minutes before, they had been making passionate love in the dark. Loren was sipping a cold Pabst as he thought of her.

Beverly's sexual intensity had not waned after their marriage, as he expected. Their time together was still like the emotional discoveries they had made in the Philippine jungle. Her deep love for him was what it was all about, the force that impelled the love he felt for her in turn.

He spoke to her, as she lay curled up under his arm. "I talked to the Navy Department this week. It looks like the O.S.S. might not be long for this world and I felt that I needed to see what my options were."

"What did they say?"

"They want me to become part of Naval Intelligence. They fully realize what we have been through, and they are offering a three-year stint of shore duty based right here in Washington."

"Oh, Loren, that would be wonderful! I would like so much to have a real home here." Beverly had been highly selective in her search for furnishings for the house and she told him, just recently, that they probably had what they needed to start a basic household.

Her two most recent finds had been a working refrigerator and a set of furnishings for a child's room.

"I think I'll have a talk with Pat McFadden next week and get his input on the situation. You know, the President has made public remarks that he doesn't see the need to continue our function. I think that what has landed on him is so overwhelming that he hasn't really thought it out. The Russians are starting to give us trouble already. If the O.S.S. goes, we will be blind as far as international intelligence."

"You're in the best position to know what to do, Loren. Whatever comes, I think it would be a good idea for us to establish a permanent home."

"I want that too, Bev. I think we'll know really soon what's going to happen."

The politicking and lobbying continued through the end of summer, in an effort to bolster support for a centralized intelligence capability. Loren found that many people like himself, military men assigned to the O.S.S., were actively campaigning for its survival. In addition, a great number of former O.S.S. personnel were pitching in as well. General Donovan had mounted a public relations campaign to inform the public and elected officials about the O.S.S. contributions during the late war. As a part of this campaign, they released the full story of Loren's activities in the Philippines for general consumption. The Washington Post gave an excellent serialized account of the years behind Japanese lines.

When they met for golf that weekend, Bob and Cara Lee were bursting with congratulations. "I had no idea that you had done all those things in the Philippines while you were there. I sort of guessed that there was more to it than what we previously read, but wow!"

"We just did what we could, Bob. You would have done the same thing, or something like it."

"The important thing is that you went out and did it. Cara Lee and I are really impressed!" Uncomfortable with all the praise, Loren switched the topic of their conversation to their golf that morning. Playing the great game, as Rudyard Kipling had so aptly put it, always seemed to fascinate people.

Despite the efforts of many, President Truman on September 20, 1945 signed a dissolution order for the O.S.S. The R & A Branch became part of the State Department, while all clandestine activities were now the responsibility of the War Department. Many now former O.S.S. employees felt they had been ill-used and insufficiently appreciated by the government. In response to some vague wordings in the dissolution order, the State Department said that they would work out a long-term solution to the central intelligence problem. Loren thought that this situation was unworkable, with the analysis function organizationally separate from its source of raw field data. He began preparations to resume his naval career.

A week later, there was an O.S.S. wide party at the Riverside Skating Rink on Rock Creek Drive to honor General Donovan. The rink itself was at the foot of the hill below O.S.S. Headquarters. The large number of attendees, many in uniform, were subdued. The O.S.S. had acquired many military types for its ranks. Most of them were now just staying to perform an orderly shutdown before returning to their respective services. When Loren and Beverly first arrived, they didn't see anyone they knew at first. Then they ran into Tom Kite, who was with a redhead this time.

A short time later, Pat McFadden and his wife arrived. Pat saw Bev and Loren and made his way over to them. "My wife is over there talking to one of her cronies. She'll be along presently. Tell me, are you still dead set on going back to the Navy?"

"I think it's the best thing for me, Pat. With the organization the politicians have handed us, I think centralized intelligence is a dead issue for the foreseeable future."

"I know what you mean, but what you see now is not necessarily what you'll see a few months from now. Ah, here comes my wife. Come see me tomorrow and I'll fill you in." Loren knew in his heart of hearts that, if there was any possibility of continuing his career in the dynamic atmosphere he had been part of these past months, he wanted to do it. They exchanged pleasantries with the McFaddens for a few minutes, before the formal part of the evening got under way.

Loren stopped by Pat's office first thing Monday morning. They decided to get together a couple of hours hence in a small conference room, where they wouldn't be disturbed. They closed the door behind them and Pat started out. "Everyone who knows anything about the intelligence game knows how important it is to have a centralized data gathering and analysis function. Because we don't have that now, it's going to become very apparent in the next months that this organization, as it is now, is not going to work.

"Those of us who have worked this side of the street these past few years are forming an organization whose purpose is to promote central intelligence. It's called the Veterans of Strategic Service and has both current and former O.S.S. people as members. Their tasks are to continue lobbying for a centralized intelligence function and do whatever else they can to make this happen. We'd like you to be a part of it too. Once this administration sees how important it is going to be to have first hand intelligence information on the Soviet Union, then things will start to happen."

"What about General Donovan?"

"He's resigned as Head of the O.S.S. I don't know how much of a factor he is going to be in the future."

Loren considered a moment. "Yeah, Pat, I'm your man."

CHAPTER XVIII—THE WAR DEPARTMENT

Loren told Beverly about his decision that evening. "I'm glad, Loren. I think you have really enjoyed working in this environment and you'd miss it if you had to do something that was the same, day after day. What's really wonderful to me is now we can settle down with some long term prospects and not live out of a suitcase any more."

"Are you going to find a house for us?"

"Starting tomorrow!"

Bev was like a genie let out of a bottle. She found a realtor to work with and every evening she had multiple photos and descriptions to show him. They were fortunate in having a large nest egg for people their age. Almost three years of back pay for each of them amounted to quite a lot. They were in a position to buy a very nice piece of real estate.

When he came home that Friday evening, she looked as though she had a big secret. "I've found it, Loren. It's just perfect." Her smile was lovely.

"Where are the description and the photograph?"

"You've got to see it. We'll go tomorrow morning."

"What about our golf game?"

"I called and canceled."

The house was in a really nice area in Chevy Chase. That was enough to sell Loren, who was tired of the long commute from Ft. Meyer. It was a two-story white saltbox style, with an enclosed porch on one side with louvered windows. When they went inside, Loren found that the house had three bedrooms and a den, a large living room and a formal dining room. The kitchen was electric, with a walk-in pantry. French Doors led from the living room onto the side porch, already furnished with a lawn swing, wood framed lawn furniture and a low table. A ten-foot-high laurel hedge surrounded the spacious back yard. The attached single car garage had an entry through the kitchen.

They strolled around the immediate neighborhood, looking at the other houses from the point of view of potential residents. A block and a half away was a small business area, with two grocery stores and a meat market, a shoemaker, a variety store, a bakery and a hole in the wall type coffee shop. In front of the shoemaker's shop was a bus stop for service to downtown Washington. Loren would have to return his car to the motor pool and look for a replacement once they left Ft. Meyer, so this was welcome.

They spent their next few days with various agencies, doing the paper work to become homeowners. Then Loren took some days off to move their possessions into the house, more or less where they envisioned them.

"I had a hell of a time arranging for drayage to transport your cache of furniture and appliances from downtown Washington out to Chevy Chase," he told Bev. "Apparently, everyone is moving somewhere."

"We still have to make some trips out to Ft. Meyer to get the rest of our things."

"I know. I'm not looking forward to it." After the better part of a week, they finished moving in, more or less. Many large cardboard boxes still stood in various corners of the rooms, but there was time for that later.

On their second night in the house, when they were deliciously naked in bed, Beverly put her arms around his neck and looked into his eyes. "Loren, please don't…" she paused, "don't pull away any more." Her smile was angelic.

The following Monday, Loren officially began his career as a civilian employee of the War Department. They were working in the same building where they had been members of the O.S.S., at least for the present. After attrition from the military reassignments, the Strategic Services Unit, of which he was part, stood at about seven hundred fifty people, though the actual number was secret. The Philippine Islands Operations Department was no more. His job description classified him as one of the P.I. experts, along with some of the people from MacArthur's former staff. He filed his application for a commission in the Naval Reserve on inactive status and hoped that he had made the right decision.

On his second day there, McFadden poked his head into Loren's office. "You'd better check the bulletin board. The Jap POW lists have just come in."

Loren got up quickly from his chair and hurried to the front of the building. The thick listing hung from a clipboard. He searched quickly through the S's and found what he hoped would be there. JoAnne's name was on a list from a camp in southern Honshu. Then he saw Tom Kite standing beside him.

"I saw her name just a couple of minutes ago. There's four of the 28 boat's crew too."

"Thank God. I was hoping against hope." Loren called their new number in Chevy Chase from his office. Beverly answered immediately. "Bev, they have posted the Jap POW lists. JoAnne is on it."

"Oh, Loren!" For a moment, there was silence. "Do you think you can get an address? I want to write her."

"I'll see what I can do."

One of the Research and Analysis people called him a few days later. "Commander, I got that address you asked for, the one for the nurse POW. I also got some dope about her from the debriefs. It isn't very nice."

"What do you mean?"

"Well, the Japs were pretty angry after the shellacking they took. The commanding officer paraded her before his troops and called her a whore. Then he gave her to them. She was in their hands for quite awhile and was raped repeatedly."

Loren was close to being sick to his stomach. "How is she now?"

"Well, when she arrived at the prison camp on Honshu, she was in pretty bad shape, but they had some medical people who were prisoners as well who helped her. She recovered pretty well physically based on the information we have, but she has some serious mental problems. That's all I have, sir. Oh, that Jap commander is on the war criminals list. He had a history of that kind of thing."

Loren fought the feeling of nausea that came over him again. After a long silence, he responded. "Thank you for the input," he managed and then hung up. He decided that he wouldn't tell Bev about the worst of it. He gave her JoAnne's address at the Veteran's Hospital that night.

"Why is she still in a hospital, Loren?"

"She's in a mental ward, Bev. She has had a bad time."

"How bad, Loren?"

"Very bad. You'll have to watch what you say to her when you write. You might even want to wait awhile before you do."

"No, I want to write her now. We were very close, you know. I'll be careful what I say."

They settled into their routine, day-to-day life that was so different from the tempestuous times that they had lived through. Loren had the fuel oil for their furnace topped off, but they found themselves in the middle of a beautiful Indian Summer and didn't have to run it at all. Bob and Cara Lee threw them a surprise housewarming the following weekend and they received a number of nice gifts.

In the evenings, they would sit in the lawn swing on the enclosed porch with the windows open and listen to the hum of the cicadas in the trees. "It's going to be so nice in the summer," Bev was saying. "We could put up a badminton court in the back yard, or maybe set up for some croquet when we entertain next summer."

"Looking forward to it. The house is really shaping up. Hey, before the winter sets in, why don't we go out to the Shenandoah Valley to see the fall colors? We've got the car from Ft. Myers for one more weekend before I have to turn it in."

"You're on!"

With the fall, Loren and Beverly found that life in Washington was slowly reverting to peacetime. The government had stopped printing ration coupons and curtailed the activities of the Office of Price Administration. Loren had had no luck in locating an automobile that he would care to own and was looking forward to the display of '46 Fords that was opening the next week.

An article in the Post told about a decision to reinstate the free concerts at the Watergate, near the Lincoln Memorial, in September. The article mentioned that the National Symphony Orchestra had played there before the war, along with some well-known military bands. The other sure sign of the easing of wartime controls was galloping inflation.

The warm sun was still shining on an October Saturday, and Loren had opened the front door to enjoy it while he could. Bev was at her hair appointment and he was examining his nonclassified read file from work. He was deep into a report on Philippine economic development when the front doorbell rang.

"Come on in, I'm back here in the den." He was just finishing the long paragraph on hemp production when he felt soft hands on his shoulders. A wisp of hair brushed his cheek and he turned to find Cara Lee looking intently over his shoulder.

"Now what's this that you are so involved in?" He felt her breasts press against him.

Loren turned in his chair as he rose to his feet, taking her in his arms as he did. Cara Lee was wearing a golf skirt and a jersey pullover that accentuated her striking figure. He looked into her eyes as she pressed against him, putting her arms around his neck. "I don't like to play games, Cara Lee."

"Neither do I." He felt her tongue in his mouth as they embraced.

Loren took her by the hand and led her into the guest bedroom next to the den. They kissed again with elemental passion. Her pullover and skirt were on the floor and then her undergarments.

He picked her up and carried her to the bed. She lay on the white spread, watching him as he undressed. Then, he was beside her, touching her. "You are so beautiful," he said.

They clung together in a desperate, frantic embrace as they loved. Afterwards, he held her in his arms, caressing her until desire quickly returned. The ecstasy they felt was overpowering.

They lay side by side on the bed, sated. The afternoon sun shone through the gauze curtains. Cara Lee toyed with the bullet scar on his arm. "There was something about you from the very first. A sense of...well...danger, violence. You're not like Bob, are you? You're one of those who goes out in the field."

"You know I can't tell you anything about that."

"I know...but you are, aren't you?" Loren said nothing. Instead he pulled her to him and kissed her once more. Her soft arms held him. Suddenly, she pulled away. "I've got to go! Bev will be coming back from her hair appointment and here we are stark naked!" She got up and started searching for her lingerie. After watching her for a moment, Loren rose as well. They dressed and he walked with her to the still open door. They stood in the doorway for a moment and she looked into his eyes. "I have a confession to make. I knew about Bev's hair appointment. That's why I came over."

"I'm very glad you did." They kissed once more, and then she was gone.

Loren thought about his afternoon with Cara Lee as he went through the routine of his workweek. He knew that trysts like the one they experienced meant nothing to her and he knew that, if Bob was aware of it, he probably would not care particularly either. Loren found it impossible to dismiss the experience. Shaken by his desire for her, he didn't know what to do.

The fall had finally come, with its inclement weather, and they put up their golf clubs for the season. Loren's winter athletic activity was handball, so they saw less of Bob and Cara Lee. When they did meet, it required an enormous effort on his part to appear relaxed and nonchalant. Cara Lee would look at him, and she knew. He thought it might be that way for her as well.

At a Christmas party at their Division Head's home, Loren and Bev ran into Bob and Cara Lee for the first time in quite awhile.

Bob introduced them to another couple. "Loren, Bev, I'd like you to meet Ray and Sue Hauscheldt."

Loren shook Ray's hand. "It's a pleasure." Bev said hello and they spoke for a few minutes. The Hauscheldts were both of medium height, young, personable and very attractive. Sue had beautiful long, blonde hair. They didn't see Bob and Cara Lee for a long time after that.

Loren became thoroughly engrossed in his work, more than he ever had before. Pat McFadden assigned him the job of liaison with the Philippine Islands contingent in the United States. In this role, he met and interfaced with members of the Philippine Mission. The Philippine Government would elevate the mission to embassy status when the Islands became independent in 1946.

He also became acquainted with Carlos Romulo who was the permanent delegate for the Philippine Government to the United Nations and Resident Commissioner of the Philippines in Washington. Like many Filipinos, Romulo was short in stature and thin. Loren towered over him. Through Romulo, Loren gained much inside information on the state of the Philippine Nation, at least from the government's point of view.

They were meeting again that morning. "There is a nationwide feeling of euphoria, Commander, with the day of independence coming closer. Despite the devastation, there doesn't seem to be a problem of any magnitude that we can't solve in time. The population is behind the democratic process and their participation in it. I would like to see you come to the Philippines on a regular basis to see for yourself what the situation is."

"I'd very much like to do that."

"To start with, I would like to invite you to participate in the Philippine Independence ceremonies that will take place on July 4. I'll make it official with your people in the next day or two."

"Thank you very much, Mr. Commissioner. I can't think of a better way to get started." He was excited about the prospect and looked forward to returning to the Islands, now that they were at last at peace.

In an afternoon meeting, they discussed problems that they needed to deal with. Romulo was speaking in the small conference room. "There are really only two issues that need a decision up front.

The first is the immense amounts of military equipment, arms, ammunition, construction material and even food left by the U.S. military in the Islands. The Americans were anticipating a longer war. The Philippines were a jumping off point for the invasion of the Japanese mainland. The war materiel is stored in warehouses scattered along the length of the island chain, and there is no apparent central control. I'm afraid that a lot of it may end up being funneled to the communists."

"I'll raise the issue with U.S. military authorities regarding the disposition of all of that. We wouldn't want to see it passed into the wrong hands."

"The other issue is the reluctance of the leftist guerrillas, who have fought so valiantly against the Japanese, to give up their arms as the central government has ordered. Some of these guerrillas are openly communistic, with all that implies."

"I don't see an immediate solution to that, Mr. Commissioner, other than to make sure the government's soldiers are trained and equipped and ready to deal with potential trouble from the guerrillas. We will do our part to see that this happens."

At the conclusion of their series of meetings, Loren decided to talk to Romulo about Ramon and Tomi. "Mr. Commissioner, I would like to request that the Philippine Government help me in a personal matter. I need to locate some people I knew during the war."

"I had heard that you were looking for some of those from the days when we fought the Japanese. It would help me if you could tell me more about them." Loren told him the story of those incredible days and the firefight with the Japanese troops. "And you have not seen or heard of Ramon and Tomi since?"

"That's right. It would mean a great deal to me if I could find them again."

"Is it true that the girl Tomi was carrying your child?"

"Yes, that is true." Loren thought that Romulo knew a lot of things.

"I will see what I can find out."

CHAPTER XIX—MANILA

The political struggle for the structuring and control of intelligence activities in the U.S. never waned and, in January of 1946, the Strategic Services Unit, of which Loren was a part, became the Office of Special Operations. The Head of OSO reported to a newly created organization, the Central Intelligence Group. The Central Intelligence Group reported via a Director of Central Intelligence to the newly created National Intelligence Authority, which was composed of the Secretaries of State, War, and Navy, plus a personal representative of the President. McFadden was right when he told Loren that things would change for the better.

Beverly and Loren's life in Chevy Chase was more or less routine, now that the house was shipshape. On Saturday morning, before their golf match, Loren took a moment to look around. "You know, Bev, I think we have finally got everything where it should be now. I don't see any cardboard boxes or items of furniture hidden away because we don't know where to put them."

Bev smiled a glowing smile. "It is nice to have a place for everything. Arranging the household has been a labor of love for me."

Loren laughed. "I'm going to have to start going back to the gym. I haven't had to because, with all this moving things around, I've been working like a stevedore whenever I'm home."

They had recently become the proud owners of a new 1946 Ford. Loren gave Bev a walkaround, telling her all about the car's features. "Actually, there's not a lot that's new about the '46 Ford, Bev. It's basically a reworked '42 model. Still, there's always something great about a new car, with the new car smell inside and everything in top-notch working order."

"That's all true, I suppose. The best part is, we're much more mobile now. We can even go for rides on weekends."

Recently, Pat McFadden and his wife Ellen were dinner guests and the two couples had a thoroughly enjoyable evening. Impressed by Loren's invitation to the Philippine Independence festivities, Pat was voluble. "An invitation from the top man! That's good work, my boy!"

"Well, we've been working pretty closely for some time now. The idea is for me to see firsthand what's going on in the Philippines by periodic trips and briefings. This looked like a good one to lead off on."

"Let's hope that's all they'll need us for," Pat reflected. "There's been a lot of rumors of communist agitation in central Luzon recently."

Loren was making final preparations for his trip to Manila when Tom Kite stepped into his office. "Got a minute, Loren?"

"Sure. Come on in and sit down."

Tom sat in his visitor's chair. "Loren, I got a letter from Felice."

"Hey, that's wonderful. I know you've been waiting a long time."

"Things are not real good for her now. I want to do something up front to help her. I also thought about flying back over there so that we could get married. What do you think?"

"Are you sure that's what you want to do?"

"Loren, I love her!"

"Do you think she would be happy here? It's not much of a statement for our society, but she would never be accepted."

"What about Tomi, Loren?"

139

Loren reflected for a minute. "I loved her very much. If I could have found her, things might have been different. If I found her today, I would do what I could to help, but I don't think she would have been happy here. If she survived, we'd have a child now, and the child would not be accepted either. I think things are changing so that it might not be that way in a few years, especially here in the East, but for now that's how it is."

"So, we'd be social outcasts!" he said angrily. After a minute or so, he spoke again. "I guess I need to think about this a lot more. Thanks for the shoulder, Loren."

"You know that I'm going to be in Manila next week. Is there anything I can do on the spot over there?"

"I have to think what I'm going to do first."

"If you decide that you want to bring Felice to the United States, Bev and I will help in any way we can."

"Thanks again, Skipper." Tom walked away, deep in thought.

Loren talked to Beverly that night about Tom's letter from Felice.

"Now isn't that strange. Loren, I heard from JoAnne today."

"Really! What did she say?"

"Only that she was surprised to hear from us and surprised that we were married. She sends her best to both of us. She seems quite normal."

"Thank God. I hope she's really all right."

"I'll write her back tomorrow. She says that she would like to keep in touch."

After a long, uneventful trip, Loren checked into the Manila Hotel two days before the scheduled festivities. Only one floor of rooms was available because of the extensive war damage and there was not a vacant one. He reflected on the history of this famous building as he rode up in the elevator. The luxurious penthouse that had been on the top of the hotel was gone, destroyed during the fighting. It was the residence of General Douglas MacArthur, before the war, and the Japanese commander had lived there for awhile during the occupation.

The Manila Hotel's famous Fiesta Pavilion was extensively damaged in the war, but had already hosted the first post war social event. The hotel management draped the structural damage to the Pavilion with parachute silk until repairs were completed. Still, the hotel itself was the center of activity in the city, except for the Malacanang Palace, the seat of government of newly elected President Roxas.

The following morning, a presidential limousine picked Loren up at the hotel and transported him to the Palace. He spent the day meeting members of the Philippine Government and renewing old acquaintances with some of his comrades from the war, most of who were now in the military.

Independence Day for the Philippine Islands was a spectacular sight. Over 200,000 people crowded Luneta Park in the center of Manila to watch the ceremonies. President Roxas took the oath of office as a brisk wind caused the flags to snap in place. Paul McNutt, representing the U.S. Government, read the proclamation of Philippine independence. The population responded with a loud roar. Loren was standing close to the reviewing stand where General of the Armies Douglas MacArthur watched the proceedings. MacArthur's reception from the Philippine people was tremendous.

As the solemn ceremonies proceeded, Loren gazed around him at the shattered buildings of Manila that were visible from where he stood. The sixteenth century walled city of Intramuros, to the north, was nothing but rubble. The business district to the south was much the same. He had heard estimates that upwards of seventy percent of the city was still in ruins. The war was not that far away on that July day in 1946. Loren reflected that he himself had had a Japanese mandated price on his head quite recently.

The climax of the day was the flag raising ceremony, in which a color guard lowered the U.S. flag and then raised the new Philippine flag to the top of the flagstaff. Buoyed by the festive mood of the city, Loren made his way back to the hotel to prepare for the celebrations of the evening.

The government hosted the gala of all galas at the Malacanang Palace that night. The splendor of the furnishings and decor was striking as he entered the main ballroom of the palace. Carlos Romulo motioned him to join his group at a table set with the finest of linens, china, crystal and silverware. They enjoyed course after course of the most succulent cuisine. The accompanying wines, mostly from Europe, were of the best vintages. Romulo's table included the majority of the diplomatic corps that would represent the new nation in Washington. They talked with fervor about the bright future in store for their country.

Loren excused himself from the opulent table after conversing with the Philippine diplomats for a considerable time. He was glad to be able to exercise his Tagalog again. He had not had the opportunity for some time, because the contingent in Washington insisted on speaking English in all of their meetings. He walked to the bar to get a fresh scotch and, as he sipped, he took in the panorama of the huge celebration as it unfolded. The orchestra played popular tunes as the dancers whirled. Loren recognized some tunes from "Oklahoma."

All of the men who weren't in uniform were in white tie formal, as was he. The women wore gorgeous ball gowns and Loren was aware that this was the crème de la crème of Islands society. A beautiful young Filipino girl, holding court across the room from him, drew his attention. She was wearing a ravishing, champagne colored gown and the young men were literally swarming around her. He guessed that she was about eighteen or nineteen. There's really nothing quite like being young and beautiful, he thought as he watched her.

The girl turned and caught his eye. He held her gaze for a moment. Then she excused herself from the circle of young men about her and walked toward him across the room. She made a sweeping bow in front of him. "May I have this dance, Commander Middleton?"

Loren was speechless. He finally managed an affirmative and they were out on the floor in the whirl of dancers. They politely applauded at the end of the light quick music. A slow dance followed and she stayed by his side. The lights dimmed as they danced.

Loren held her closely. "You have the advantage of me. How do you come to know who I am?"

"I am Maria Castillejos, and your fame has preceded you."

"Fame? What fame?"

"My father pointed you out and told me of your part in the war against the Japanese. He is in the diplomatic corps now, but he was with Colonel Kangleon."

Loren seemed to remember the name as one of the Colonel's officers. "That was a long time ago. Tell me, are you enjoying the evening?"

"Much more so now." A young man who wanted to cut in interrupted them. "Enjoyed meeting you, Commander. Save me a dance for later." She was gone in the crush on the dance floor.

They danced several more times that evening. When he looked for her in the crowd, she would leave her audience and come to him. When the festivities ended, Loren made his way back to his room at the Manila Hotel with a good feeling inside. The attention he received from the young girl was flattering, though probably politically motivated. Carlos Romulo, who had accompanied him to the hotel, joked with him about his conquest. After all of the day's activities, he fell into a deep sleep.

The next few days were a succession of meetings and briefings concerning all aspects of the Philippine Islands. In one of these meetings, he renewed his association with the legendary leader of the guerrilla army on Leyte, Ruperto Kangleon, who was now the Defense Secretary of the Philippine Government.

Loren strode forward to take his hand. "Hello, Colonel. It's been a long time."

"Commander Middleton! It's a great pleasure to see you again. We all remember your brave deeds from those dark days of the occupation." They went on to talk of the people they had known. "Do I understand correctly that you and the navy nurse Lieutenant Jones are now man and wife?"

"Yes, sir, since two years ago."

"Congratulations, and please convey my best wishes to her. Tell her I remember her and all that she did for us."

"I will do that. Thank you, Colonel."

CHAPTER XX—CHEVY CHASE

In the third week in July, Loren arrived back in the United States. The Pan Am Clipper landed at San Francisco Airport at the end of the long, tiring flight from Manila. After clearing customs, Loren spent the night at the St. Francis to rest and get his internal clock back in order. The following morning, he boarded an American Airlines DC-4 for the flight to Washington, D.C. via Chicago, arriving at Washington's National Airport in the early evening.

Beverly was waiting for him and she rushed into his arms as he came into the terminal. He had never seen her so exuberant. "Hello, darling. Welcome home!"

"It's good to be here."

An hour later, they were home and Loren poured himself a scotch as he described his trip to Bev. She seemed preoccupied as they talked. "The bad thing about all of this travel is that we've missed half of the golf season. Have you been getting out with Cara Lee?"

"Not for the past two weeks. Loren, sit down a minute. I've something to tell you."

"OK."

"We're going to be parents next March."

"My God!" He leapt to his feet and went to her. "That's wonderful! When did you find out?"

"About two weeks ago."

"Why didn't you call me?"

"I figured it would keep." He held her in his arms.

They spent the next hour talking and making plans. Loren was excited. "Isn't this something! Did the doctor say anything?"

"Only that I have to be a little careful. Apparently, I don't have an ideal build for child bearing."

"You better listen and take care of yourself."

"I will, darling."

Loren had just walked into his office when the phone rang. Pat wanted to see him immediately. He headed down to Pat's posh corner office.

Pat looked up as Loren entered the office. "Welcome back! You've got to tell me all about your trip."

They spent the next hour and a half talking, as Loren gave him a rundown on the various happenings. He left out the part about the girl, Maria. With Pat's propensity for humor, he wasn't about to give him any ammunition. When he had finished, Loren sat back in his chair. "Anything new on this end?"

"Well, we've had some things happen while you were gone. Tom Kite has resigned."

"No! Did he say why?"

"He said it was for personal reasons. I thought maybe you could shed some light on it."

"He mentioned to me just before I left that he had heard from a girl in the Philippines who had meant a lot to him during the time we were on Leyte. He was talking about marriage. I'm not sure if that has anything to do with it or not."

"If you hear from him, please let me know. There is always concern when someone with his level of clearance leaves the fold. Just from a personal point of view, I'd like to know too. I always thought he had a lot of promise."

"If I hear anything, I'll pass it along."

About two months later, Bev and Loren received a letter from Tom in the Philippines telling them about his marriage to the girl Felice and his intentions to remain there. Loren heard officially much later that Tom was working for the Philippine Government in an antiguerrilla unit.

145

In their weekly meeting in the large conference room, Pat presented an update on the Philippine situation. "The people downtown are getting stirred up about the communist guerrilla movement in a big way. In their haste to support anti-Japanese guerrillas during the late war, many government officials did not stop to consider that those they supported might be pro-communists. The tough thing about it is that they fought well against the Japanese in the war, but now they're the bad guys. Their increase in power and influence has come about because of alleged injustice, corruption and misgovernment of elected officials in the Central Government of the Philippines.

"They call themselves Huks, or Hukbalahap, which is short for Hukbo ng Bayan Laban so Hapon, or People's Army to Fight the Japanese. Lately, they've been calling themselves Hukbong Magpapalaya ng Bayan, the Army of Liberation of the People. Whatever their title, a Huk is still a Huk. It's difficult at this time to determine whether their motivation is communist ideology or the malfeasant activities of the Central Government, as they proclaim.

"Their power base is in Central Luzon, where conditions appear to be especially ripe for their influence. Loren Middleton, back there in the corner has inherited this bag of snakes." Loren stood up and raised his hand. "Do you have anything to add, Loren?"

"Only that it's not getting any better."

The reports that Loren was receiving on the Huks were not encouraging. They seemed to be getting stronger and gaining more popular support. He wondered what he would find when he traveled to the Philippines after the first of the year. He was more concerned about leaving Bev for a long period of time. Her pregnancy had not been an easy one so far and she had not been feeling well at all. They went to bed early that warm August night, because he was tired and Bev was sleeping a great deal these days.

Well past midnight, Loren awoke suddenly to find their bedclothes soaking. Bev was having spasms of pain. My God, he thought, the baby! He threw on his sweat suit and wrapped Beverly in her robe before carrying her down to the car. In fifteen minutes, they arrived at the local hospital and he hurriedly parked at the emergency exit. The next few minutes were a blur, as he formally signed Bev in for admittance and then watched a nurse wheel her away into the emergency room. Then it was waiting, for a long time.

Finally, the on call doctor came into the waiting room. Loren was on his feet. "Your wife is all right, Mr. Middleton. However, she has lost the child."

"I thought maybe that was what had happened. Will she be OK when this is over?

"She should be. The problem is her uterus. It's tipped, and there has been some damage. Given a few days rest in the hospital, she should heal naturally."

Loren was tired and dispirited as he drove back to their home. Bev and he had looked forward so much to having a child, and now it was all snatched away from them. After he arrived home, he poured himself a scotch and sat in their darkened living room staring into the gloom. He thought about the events of the night. This is not the end of everything, he said to himself, only a small setback. We can have other children. He rose and stretched, and then went upstairs to their bedroom. He realized that he was there alone for the first time. He slept a restless sleep.

When the doctor allowed him to see Beverly, he found that she was under sedation and was not fully aware of what was going on around her. During the third day, she finally realized what had happened. After a week and a half, the doctor released Bev from the hospital. Loren parked at the emergency exit again and helped her to the car. Her strength returned gradually in the succeeding days and she appeared to be physically back to normal.

Beverly was terribly depressed over losing the child and Loren stayed close by her, to love her and to comfort her. She had little to say and did not return the affection that he showed her. By the holidays, three months later, she seemed to be a bit better, but Loren wondered how much she might be holding inside. He saw little change in her condition as they started the New Year.

Beverly went back to the doctor's office on a weekly basis for the next month. After the last visit, she seemed even more depressed and down. After dinner that evening, they talked. "What is it, Bev? Please tell me what it is that's bothering you."

"Oh, Loren!" She could not hold back the tears any longer. He held her in his arms as she sobbed. After a few minutes, she regained control. "Loren, I can't have children any more."

He had never seen her this way before. "Is that what the doctor told you?"

"Yes."

Loren absorbed this for a minute or two. "So, it's not the end of the world. We can always adopt, you know."

"It's not the same."

"I've known a lot of couples who could not have children. They have adopted one or more youngsters and are very happy with their families."

"It doesn't matter to you then?"

"Of course not. We can start looking into what's needed to adopt right away."

"I'd like to think about it, Loren. Give me some time."

"Whatever you want, darling. We've been through much too much together to let something like this slow us down." He held her tenderly in his arms.

In the ensuing weeks, Beverly became increasingly withdrawn and had even less to say. They had no marriage at all anymore and Loren was at a loss as to what to do. All the warmth seemed to have drained from her. With his extended stay in the Philippines growing closer, he was concerned about her.

He talked with her doctor about what was happening. He was not encouraging. "This kind of thing is not uncommon when a woman miscarries. She has had a double shock, because now she can't have any more children. All we can do is wait and hope that she works this out on her own. There is always therapy, of course, but I would like to wait for awhile before recommending that."

Finally, he talked with her when he was within a month of his planned departure date. "Bev, I think I will cancel out on this trip to the Philippines. I need to be here with you."

"Oh, that's all right, Loren." She showed no emotion. "I'll be fine here. You need to make this trip. It's your job."

"Are you sure?"

"Yes." He kissed her lightly as he held her. She did not respond.

Loren suggested that they call Bob and Cara Lee and do something, but Bev showed no interest. Her bouts of depression continued during the remaining cold, wet days of February. He remembered her way of withdrawing when things were difficult in the past. After six months, the warm loving person he had known was a memory.

At first, he thought that he would be the strong one, the one who would help her to overcome her problems. Instead, he was drug down into the morass himself. The strain was beginning to tell on him at work, where he was impatient and short with others.

In March, as he prepared for his trip to the Philippines, he watched Bev for some sign of improvement, but saw none. He felt very much alone. She was like a different person and Loren wondered about the future. He resolved to talk to her doctor again.

When he went to see Dr. Marcus, the doctor had many questions for him. After an hour or so, Dr. Marcus sat back in his chair. "If you were going to be here, I might recommend a different direction, but now, I feel that your wife would benefit by a visit to a sanitarium and some extensive therapy."

"I can cancel this trip if necessary, Doctor."

"No, on reflection, I feel that some undivided time on her part to address her problems is the best approach. I want to see her again in the next day or two. I'll explain to her what we have discussed."

On the following weekend, Loren drove Bev to the sanitarium in Northern Virginia. She was withdrawn and had little to say.

CHAPTER XXI—RELATIONSHIPS

In mid March, Loren boarded an American Airlines flight to San Francisco, where he made ongoing connections on Pan Am to Manila. After overnighting in Honolulu at the Royal Hawaiian, he continued on, via Wake Island and Guam, to the Philippines. Flying to the Philippines was, he thought, a long, long haul. A small contingent from the Government met him and eased him through customs. By the time he had checked into the Manila Hotel, he had time only for a nightcap before weariness overtook him.

The next morning he was due to have an in-depth briefing on the Huks, their organization, suspected motives and future actions. The army officer who gave the presentation had recently returned from Central Luzon, where operations were underway against Huk formations in the surrounding mountains.

"The Huks are no ragtag, undisciplined mob. On the contrary, they have been in existence since the war against the Japanese and have developed a regular army-like organization of their forces, with their basic unit called a squadron. Typically, a squadron has 100 men, divided into platoons and squads. Two squadrons form a battalion, and two battalions a regiment."

Loren addressed the presenter. "T. E. Lawrence said that a successful guerrilla campaign has to have a population base that it can fall back on. How do these Huks stack up with the people?"

"They are gaining adherents rapidly because they are selling themselves as saviors of the people, the poor and downtrodden. They are making the most trouble in Pampanga Province, where there are many large estates and absentee landlords. The peasants in that area feel that the Central Government is there only to support the landlords.

"The Huks are against the things you would expect a communist organization to be against, the Military Base Agreement with the U.S. and the proposed trade agreement with the U.S., the Bell Act. There is going to be a referendum on the trade agreement in a special election and the Huks are actively campaigning against its acceptance." The presenter went on to give an in-depth analysis of the political issues confronting them. At the end of the session, they announced a briefing on the Huk leadership for the next day.

Loren was glad for the busy work schedule, because it took his mind away from the difficult personal situation he had at home. Thousands of miles away and involved in a dynamic job situation requiring his utmost concentration and ability, it was just what he needed. He had some hard lifetime decisions to make, but for now, he could put them out of his mind and concentrate on the problems at hand.

He returned to the Manila Hotel quite late, after dining with the Filipino contingent from Washington. In his mailbox, he found an embossed envelope. Much to his surprise, it contained an invitation to a black tie formal dinner at the Castillejos' for the following evening. He thought of the girl at the Independence Gala and wondered if she had something to do with the invitation. He had nothing on his schedule, so he decided to accept.

The following morning, a detailed briefing on the leadership of the Huks concentrated on Luis Turac, their acknowledged leader, and his friend and advisor, Dr. Vincent Lava. The army officer who had presented the previous day was at the podium. "Turac originally presented himself as a socialist but, more recently, he has espoused the communist line. Dr. Lava is an out-and-out communist who has great influence on Turac. They've returned to the hills, ostensibly to fight the supposed injustices of the newly elected Central Government."

The afternoon session dealt with, to Loren, the depressing story of ineffectual government raids against the Huks. "They periodically plan raids against the Huk bases," the briefing officer intoned, "with large numbers of troops and heavy weaponry. The Huks usually know in advance that they are coming and simply melt into the jungle. The poor people of Central Luzon cooperate fully with the Huks and can easily warn them of approaching trouble. Because of the perceived ineffectiveness of the Central Government in dealing with the problems of the peasants, they in turn fully support the Huks."

That evening, Loren took a cab to the Castillejos' spacious home in the southern suburbs of Manila. He had just entered the luxurious salon when Maria came up to him.

"Commander Middleton, it's so good to see you again. Did you have a nice trip over?"

"Pleasant, but long," he replied. "It's good to see you as well."

They talked as they walked to the standup bar at the edge of the small dance floor. They drank champagne as she described the many diversions in the city of Manila. "Do you like jazz, Commander? There are a number of good jazz clubs in the city."

"Yes, I do."

"There's also some outstanding night clubs with really good shows. Just about anything you would like."

"Sounds wonderful. Would you like to dance?"

The orchestra was playing ballads and they found themselves out on the floor, swaying to the rhythm. He noticed that the partygoers were mostly older, with none of the ardent young men that had pursued Maria at the Independence Gala. The beauty and charm of the young girl drew him to her as they danced.

They stopped by to talk to his host and hostess. Loren had fleeting memories of a young man in combat fatigues during the first guerrilla offensive. "It is good to see you again, Manuel. I want to thank you for including me in your festivities tonight."

"I am honored, Commander Middleton. I hope to see more of you during your stay here in Manila."

Maria and he returned to the dance floor, mingling with the elegantly attired attendees. She was on his arm for the entire evening, introducing him to the other guests, most of whom he did not know. She joined in conversations on a wide variety of subjects, from the economy to the insurgents in the hills. From what he heard during the evening, Loren decided that both the Castillejos' and their guests were mostly liberal in outlook, both politically and socially.

Loren found again that the Filipinos knew all about the guerrilla warfare during the Japanese occupation and his role in it. He was the object of some veneration in this.

One of the guests asked him about the Huks. "Commander Middleton, as a representative of the U.S. War Department, what do you think of the government's war with the communist guerrillas?"

He replied, using his cover story. "I'm a member of the diplomatic corps and I'm here to negotiate the amount and type of military hardware to be provided by the U.S. to the Philippine Government. I have very little current knowledge of the situation here in the Philippines."

His evening with the beautiful daughter of his former comrade-in-arms ended much too soon. The time had come for him to leave when she asked him to walk with her on their terrace for a few moments. The weather was unseasonably warm as they strolled with her arm through his. "I don't know when I've enjoyed an evening so much, Maria."

"I'm glad, Loren." She turned toward him and suddenly she was in his arms. She pressed against him as they kissed, with great tenderness.

"This is so very nice, Maria," he whispered, and then they were kissing again.

After a moment, she spoke to him. "Loren, there has never been anyone in my life."

"I find that hard to understand. I remember the way it was at the Independence Gala."

"They are impetuous young men. Very young. This is not what I want."

"What, then?"

"I want you to be part of my life."

Loren was at a loss. "Why, Maria? I am years older than you, and I am married."

"I know." She looked into his eyes. "Are you happy, Loren?"

He paused for a moment. "It's a long story."

"I sensed something. I can recognize pain."

"My wife is in a sanitarium. She may never recover and be herself again."

"I'm sorry."

"It can't be helped."

"I want to be here for you, Loren. If it is meant to be, then it will all be well." Her beauty overwhelmed him as they held one another in the moonlight.

When Loren was not at the Malacanang conferences, they were inseparable. The restaurants and nightlife of Manila were especially enjoyable, with Maria at his side. On the weekends, they golfed at the exclusive Manila Golf and Country Club.

The hour was late when they came back to the Castillejos' house. They had had a marvelous evening of dinner and dancing and were in a relaxed happy mood. "Would you like a nightcap before you go, Loren?"

"That would be nice."

"It's been such a wonderful evening, I don't want it to end. Shall I pour you a scotch?"

"Yes, again." He watched her as she poured for them at the bar. Dressed in a glamorous black sheath, Maria was exquisite. She came across the room to him with their drinks.

"Here, darling." She was close beside him as they sipped.

Loren lay back on the couch, his head against the large cushions. "Where are your parents?"

"They've retired upstairs for the night. We're a little later than usual."

"And the servants?"

"They're in their quarters."

"It's not often that we are alone together."

"That's true." Then she was in his arms. Her beauty was overpowering and the sheer warmth of her excited him. The black sheath was above her waist and soft pink lingerie lay scattered at her feet. Maria looked into his eyes. "There has never been anyone, Loren."

"I know, my love, I know."

All too soon, his mission in Manila was complete and he made preparations to return to the U.S.

Maria was desolate. "When will you return, Loren?"

"We haven't made any definite plans yet, but probably sometime in the fall. It depends a lot on what is happening here." He reached out to touch her hand. "Maria, I need to tell you about my marriage."

"Yes?"

"My wife Beverly had a miscarriage a year ago and now she cannot have children. She became terribly depressed and is now suffering from acute melancholia. As I told you, I don't know if she will ever be the same again. I have been totally alone until now. I can't tell you how much it has meant to me to be here with you."

She looked into his eyes. "I'll be here when you return."

He drew her to him. "Till we can be together again, Maria."

As he settled in for the long, long flight from Manila to Honolulu, Loren was troubled. His relationship with Maria, this beautiful, intelligent young girl, was not just a harmless flirtation. They had spoken of love as they held one another in the night. He considered her youth and wondered where her heart would be six months from now. And, at home, Bev was a stranger to him, removed from his life.

He reflected on his job situation in Washington, which was in a state of flux. At the first of the year, the government added a modest research and analysis capability to his new organization. The format and procedure for passing field data to R & A was not clearly defined. Assuming that it could be cleared up, the small number of analysts meant that the final report would not be issued in a timely fashion. At the same time, the cutbacks to the field force were severe as well, so there might not be that much of a backlog of raw data. At least he didn't have to submit field data to State. Although the new organization was a clear improvement over the previous one, they had a long way to go before a multifunctional, fully capable and independent intelligence organization was in place.

Loren made an appointment with Dr. Marcus and he arrived at the doctor's office at ten o'clock. The doctor rose as Loren entered and the two men shook hands. "What do you have for me, Doctor?"

"It's too early to say yet, Mr. Middleton, but Beverly just might be turning the corner."

"She's better then?"

"Not appreciably, but there are signs. I would like to talk with you after you have visited her."

"I'm going out to see her tomorrow morning. I'll call you when I get back."

When he got to the sanitarium that morning, an attendant directed him to the courtyard, enclosed by the institution's buildings. An orderly took him out on the grounds to where Bev was resting. She saw him coming and smiled. "Hello, Loren. I'm sorry for all of this."

They embraced and then Loren looked into her eyes. "Dr. Marcus says you are making some progress."

She had on a light blue, quilted bathrobe and wore no makeup. Her face was drawn. "Yes. He tells me I am better."

They talked at length about day-to-day things, sitting in the bright sunlight. Much of her personal warmth had returned and, for the first time in a long time, he felt that he could relax in her company. She seemed to be finding her way back, a little at a time. "After you left, I made up my mind that this was not the end of the world, and that I needed to pull myself together and get on with it."

Loren was happy with how far she had come. "I've missed you, Bev."

Loren saw Bev regularly in the following weeks. The doctor had been right, he thought. Time had helped a great deal. She still had fits of depression, but it seemed to Loren that she was better every time he saw her. Loren kidded her about the great golf weather in Manila. "Got in eighteen holes every weekend I was there."

"Sounds wonderful! Who did you play with?"

"Some government people. You don't by any chance remember Manuel Castillejos? He was one of the Colonel's officers."

"No, I don't think so."

"He is in the diplomatic corps now. Many of the guerrillas that were there on Leyte are in government now. By the way, the Colonel sends his regards."

"That was nice of him."

Loren was back in his office again, as he tried to pick up the pieces of his life. When he first returned, he gave McFadden a briefing on what had happened and then started the large task of committing all the data and inputs he had received to paper. He went to the Philippine Embassy for a meeting with Romulo and some of the staff. They discussed in detail the steadily worsening situation in the Islands. Everyone was down.

They had finished their meeting at the Embassy and Loren was leaving the room when Romulo motioned to him to wait. "A moment please, Commander. We need to talk." Loren came back into the room and sat at the large table. "I have had a message from our security people in Manila. I'm sorry to say that we have been unable to find Ramon and Tomi. There has been no trace of them anywhere."

"I thought that might be the case, but I was hoping."

"The problem is the village where you were based. It doesn't exist anymore and those who lived there have moved elsewhere. There is really no one to talk to. If someone wants to disappear in that part of Mindanao, it's easy. Tomi is the daughter of a well-known guerrilla leader in that area. She would almost certainly have changed her name. Out there in that wild area, all you really have to do is say you are someone else and no one would be the wiser."

"I see. I suppose we will never know."

CHAPTER XXII—THE CENTRAL INTELLIGENCE AGENCY

Under the aggressive leadership of General Hoyt Vandenberg, the Office of Special Operations, of which Loren was part, grew dramatically by the start of 1947. Loren was spending a large part of his time interviewing potential new employees as the staffing buildup continued. OSO, his parent organization, established an office for Research and Evaluation, as well as some additional supporting administrative cadres for the entire organization. The long term goal, which Pat delineated in a paper on OSO's mission strategy, continued to be an increase in the flow of intelligence information and a centralization of the evaluation task.

At the first of the year, rumors had circulated of a reorganization of the entire military establishment that included OSO. Loren and his associates watched closely as the proposal to do this went to Congress and passed into law as the National Security Act of 1947.

General Vandenberg briefed them in the large auditorium.

"I'm sure by now that most of you have read the text of this new legislation. It means sweeping changes in how the military relates to the Government. The President has merged the War and Navy Departments to form the Department of Defense, and the Air Force is now an independent armed service. Most importantly to us, the legislation also specifies the formation of a Central Intelligence Agency. The newly created National Security Council will advise the President on defense and foreign affairs. The new intelligence agency will report to the President through the NSC."

The people in Loren's office were exuberant. One of the P.I. experts from MacArthur's command entered Loren's office with a broad smile. "Isn't this terrific, Loren? It's what we've been fighting for so long, and now it's here!"

"It does look like we're finally going to get an independent, self contained organization, even though the legislation had no specifics regarding our charter. I guess that comes later."

Loren and the others kept close track of the day-to-day business in Congress as, through the summer, they amended the legislation to specify responsibilities for the new Central Intelligence Agency in a wide variety of functions.

The day came when Dr. Marcus said that Beverly could come home. Loren was there early in the morning to bring her back to the house in Chevy Chase. She was quiet and tentative as they drove back to Washington. When they pulled into the driveway of their house, Loren saw tears glistening in her eyes. They were quiet as they entered the door. They had reached a milestone.

As the summer wore on, the anxieties of the OSO organization seemed to put a damper on social affairs and there were fewer organizational get togethers. Beverly was much better now, and Loren and she again became involved in the things that were happening.

Bob and Cara Lee were waiting for them as they walked toward the first tee. Cara Lee embraced Bev as they arrived. "It's good to see you, Bev. It's been a long while."

"Thank you. It's good to be out and about again."

Bob was beaming. "Maybe I've got a chance at winning today."

Loren smiled. "I've been playing eighteen holes every week in the Philippines. You'd better be on your mettle."

They polished their golf game against Bob and Cara Lee and a variety of other players. Loren found that, after Manila, he was no longer uncomfortable around Cara Lee. He caught her watching him when they played golf or attended events on the reduced social scene.

The planners in Washington reached agreement on the final organizational mission and structure in the summer and, in mid-September, 1947, the Central Intelligence Agency officially came into being. Amid great rejoicing at OSO, a series of raucous parties commemorated the event. Loren and Beverly received an invitation to a party thrown by the Southeast Asia Department in the immense back yard of the director's estate.

Loren brought them drinks from the bar. Beverly was sipping her gin and tonic when she looked past him at the director's house. "Loren, what is that man doing?"

He turned and saw someone balancing on a second story balcony rail. "What are you doing?" Loren called out.

The man's voice was slurred. "I'm a B-29." With that, he dove gracefully from the balcony.

Beverly's hand flew to her mouth as she cried out. She turned and buried her face against his shoulder. Loren watched, impassively. "Bev?"

"Yes?"

"He didn't fly."

She turned to look again. Relaxed from celebrating, the man got up, brushed off his clothes and unsteadily rejoined the party.

Later in the evening, Loren found himself alone with Cara Lee. She gave him a searching glance. "What's with you these days, Loren? You've got this 'I've got a secret' look."

"Hello, Cara Lee. You are looking beautiful as always. As to how I look, I don't know what you mean." He smiled at her.

"Oh, come on now! You look like Sylvester Pussycat with canary feathers in his whiskers."

"I enjoy being with you."

"Not going to tell me, huh? That's all right. I'll find out." She gave him a knowing smile.

At that moment, Bev joined them and the conversation changed to golf. A half hour later, Loren and Bev thanked their host and hostess and headed for home. "What was that all about with Cara Lee?"

"She thinks I'm looking self satisfied."

"Oh, why is that?"

"You know Cara Lee. She thinks she knows everything."

Organizational meetings filled their schedule during the next two months as the new agency took form and the holiday season was upon them before they knew it. The Philippine Islands Operations Department was back, renamed the Philippines Projects Department, and Loren was once more the head of it. This time, his management listened when he talked about training a new cadre of recruits for duty in the Philippines and Southeast Asia. He now had a head count to fill and a recruiting budget. Loren was also taking time for the study of Indochinese dialects during his busy workweek.

Bev was now drawing on her nursing skills again as a volunteer in one of the local hospitals, with the unlikely participation of Cara Lee as well. Loren thought about how high masculine morale would be when those two made the rounds.

"The Elegant and the Earthy," he mused to himself with a chuckle.

Loren and Bev started having relations again after a long, long time. In bed together, he caressed her through her nightgown. He could feel the tenseness in her body as he slid the garment down off her shoulders. It was dark in the room so he couldn't see the look in her eyes. "Are you all right, Bev?"

There was a quaver in her voice. "Yes. Loren."

Making love together was awkward at first, but things smoothed out. Their relationship felt strange to Loren after Manila. He had never stopped caring for Bev, but there had been a large void in his life when she had gone away. Then, Maria had changed everything. He wondered what he should do, now that things had changed once again.

Bev and he spent the holidays with his family, with the promise that they would go to Oregon to visit her people in the summer. They exchanged presents at his parents' house and brought in the New Year at a party given by one of the Department Heads. All in all, it was a very pleasant hiatus for both Bev and Loren before world events would overtake them again.

The news from abroad was uniformly bad as 1948 began. The reports from the Philippines that Loren read told about the Huks getting stronger and more active. In Europe, major confrontations between East and West would culminate in the Berlin Blockade and the communist takeover in Czechoslovakia. He made plans to return to the Philippines to try to deal with the latest bad news from there.

Beverly talked to him at dinner just before he left. "You know, Loren, with you gone so much, I've given some thought to going back to nursing full time. I could do some wonderful things for the house with what I earn."

"I know it's difficult, but this crisis can't go on forever. This trip should be a relatively short one. I know how you feel, so use your own judgment. Are you sure you want to go back to shift work?"

"No, I'm not, Loren, but there's not a lot for me here when you are away."

"Why don't you go out to Oregon for a while? Your family would be glad to see you."

"I'll think about it. That might not be a bad idea." Bev drove him out to National Airport the next morning.

On the long leg out from Honolulu to Manila, Loren thought again about Maria. Realistically, he probably had been the object of a young girl's infatuation when he was there last summer. He expected to arrive in Manila to find that she had long since forgotten him and was on the arm of one or more ardent suitors. The thought made him sad, though he could not expect anything else. He was glum as he deplaned from the Pan Am flight at Manila Airport. Even with his late arrival, there were Government representatives waiting for him. They whisked him through customs and on to the Manila Hotel. He was very tired as he checked in.

The hotel manager came toward him. "Mr. Middleton, I have a message for you." The familiar embossed envelope contained a dinner invitation to the Castillejos' the following evening.

He was at the Malacanang Palace the next day for meetings on the status of the Huk campaign. As he entered the grounds, he looked around him. This is not really a palace, he thought, just a number of buildings located in a parklike tropical garden. He passed the president's residence, the grand ballroom and the legislative buildings as he walked to their meeting place. The building where their briefings were was toward the rear of the grounds, behind the presidential quarters.

Loren was dismayed to find that there had been no progress in the Government's war against the guerrillas. They were still attempting large-scale confrontations with the insurgents that never materialized. Documents from some private sources he received reported that the army was simply firing off large amounts of ammunition into the jungle and then claiming large Huk casualties.

For sometime, President Roxas' American advisors had been urging an amnesty plan for the guerrillas and now, Loren learned that the president was changing his thinking and appeared to be favoring this move. The president had been in ill health for some time and Loren thought this might have been a factor in his reaching this conclusion. Suddenly, military confrontations seemed to be behind them and the Central Government was moving toward negotiations. For the first time since independence, Loren was hopeful that a solution was within reach.

CHAPTER XXIII—MARIA

He caught a cab from the front of his hotel and headed to the southern suburbs and the Castillejos' magnificent home. He wasn't quite sure what to expect when he got there.

When he entered the reception hall, Maria materialized from the library and came to him. "Loren!" she cried. Her small hands were on his arm. She drew him into a small alcove and was in his arms in an instant. The fresh smell of her hair and the feel of her in his arms were overpowering.

"Now, let's go in to see my parents and meet the rest of the guests." Her smile was dazzling. "I have a surprise for you later."

Manuel Castillejos and his wife welcomed Loren to their home. They introduced him to three couples who were in the midst of enjoying before dinner cocktails and, fortified with a martini, he entered the conversation, speaking in Tagalog.

He thoroughly enjoyed the splendid dinner with Maria at his side. The dinner conversation turned to the guerrilla war and the other guests asked him his opinion about the Huk uprising. "My role here is as an arms supplier for your military. I hope they will use the new hardware to their advantage in their confrontations with the Huks. From what I have been able to read, the Huks seem to be getting stronger."

Those at the table generally agreed and then the conversation passed on to other subjects. He did not mention the amnesty

164

negotiations, which were still in their infancy and not common knowledge.

After they left the table, Maria took Loren's arm. "We are going to go downtown for a while to take in some of the nightlife. I'm going to take the convertible, Father."

Loren thanked his host and hostess, said goodnight to their guests, and then they were on their way.

Instead of going downtown, Maria drove further south to a palatial walled villa with an ornate gate. "My aunt is in Europe for an extended stay. She said I could use her villa whenever I wanted."

They entered the elaborate front hall, and then Maria led him up the stairway to a beautifully furnished bedroom suite. Loren drew her to him. "It's been much too long, Maria."

"Yes, Loren."

They were back at her home by midnight. They sipped brandy from warmed snifters while Loren waited for his cab.

He was upbeat as he spoke. "Meet me for dinner tomorrow night. Then we'll find some good music."

"Sounds wonderful, darling, but not too late." Maria smiled. "We need our time together."

"Yes."

"Loren, how is your…wife?"

"She is better now."

"Does that mean that you no longer need me to be here for you?"

He took her in his arms and looked into her eyes.

"Perhaps we never should have met, Maria, but that is long since past. You are part of my life now and always will be."

As he rode back to the hotel, Loren thought of the evening he had just spent, as if he and Maria had never been apart. He also realized the depth of feeling he had for this beautiful young girl.

The golden days went by with a sense of euphoria, as negotiations for the proposed amnesty proceeded. Maria was there for him, as they experienced the ambiance and the vibrant nightlife of the city.

Loren wondered how Maria's parents felt about their relationship. They talked about it in the night. "I have acted as an unofficial hostess for my father many times in entertaining business and political friends of his. He and my mother aren't up to Manila nightlife any more. When you first came to our house, my father asked me to show you around Manila. They are used to me in that role and don't have second thoughts about it. Of course, they don't know about us."

"Are you sure?"

Maria was silent for a moment. "Sometimes, Mother looks at me in a certain way and I wonder if she has guessed."

Their enchanted life continued into the springtime. In years to come, he knew that he would think of this time as close to perfection.

The phone rang in his room at 3:00 A.M. and Loren fumbled for the receiver. "Yes?"

"Loren, get dressed and come to the Embassy as soon as you can. President Roxas has just died."

As he showered, the enormity of the President's death hit him. My God, he thought, of all times for the head of state to die this has to be the worst. What will happen to the amnesty now? Will everything fall apart? His mind was racing as he dressed for the Embassy meeting.

The emergency meeting finished a little after nine, and Loren left the Embassy in search of breakfast and some strong coffee. He had gotten about two hours sleep. The government cancelled all official business in honor of the late President. A state funeral and the inauguration of Vice President Quirino as the new head of state would take up the next few days. Loren cabled Bev about the indefinite extension of his stay in the Philippines. The end result of the meetings at the Embassy was disappointing. They would just go with the status quo and hope that this disruption would not harm the peace process.

At the first of the week, the guerrillas started to move down from the hills. Loren thought that they could not do anything else and retain credibility. He wondered how committed they were to really ending the hostilities. Things were in a state of suspense, as Elpideo Quirino became the new president. Then, those who had entered into the amnesty agreement in good faith and with resolve watched as little things started to go wrong.

Maria noticed his depression and wondered. "What is it, Loren? Are things really that bad?"

"It looks like it's only going to get worse, Maria. The army leaders are starting to act as though they were victors. I understand that now they are going to require the guerrillas to hand over their weapons or they will cancel the amnesty. That is not going to work."

"I'm sorry, Loren."

"I'm sorry for all of us, Maria."

With sinking hopes, Loren watched as the Huks returned to the hills and the confrontation with government forces became more savage than it had been before. Now we are for it, he thought. The chance for peace in the Philippines is gone for good.

The intelligence reports that Loren received indicated that, despite efforts to the contrary, the Huks had gained control of a large part of the weapons arsenal left at the end of the war by the Americans and were well armed. He watched as both sides with increasing frequency perpetrated terrorist acts. Disagreements within the government as to how to proceed were shrill. In meetings that Loren attended, Colonel Kangleon differed sharply with the President and his people as to how to handle the military situation. His deputy, Ramon Magsaysay, who was another former guerrilla leader, strongly supported the Colonel's position.

In the newspapers and on the radio, the Huks revived graft and corruption charges against the Central Government and, in what seemed no time at all, open warfare between the communist guerrillas and the Central Government resumed. Loren concluded that there was a need for radical action to end these hostilities and communicated his recommendation to Washington. He wondered if the answer might lie with the Defense Secretary's deputy, Magsaysay, and determined to seek him out.

Meanwhile, half a world away, a seemingly unconnected event took place. The Office of Policy Coordination, or OPC, became part of the organizational structure of the CIA. Their charter was for covert and psychological warfare.

Loren decided to leave the depressing situation that he found himself in at work. When he passed through the door of the building in which they were meeting and out into the tropical gardens on the palace grounds, he put it all behind him and thought of the evening. He had an exciting city to enjoy and a beautiful girl to enjoy it with. Still, he and Maria were spending more time at her aunt's villa than before and, surprisingly, the excitement between them was growing.

He held her in his arms, his face close to hers, her head touching his shoulder. "Maria?"

"Yes, Loren."

"I love you, Maria."

She looked into his eyes. "I know. I love you too, Loren. Do you know that also?"

"Yes, Maria, I know." He drew her to him.

As the days went by, the strength of their feelings for each other carried them along and they did not know where it would take them. Manila was their own personal city, put there just for their enjoyment. Beautiful, intelligent, educated, skilled socially, she was everything he could ever want in a woman. They became even closer as time went by.

Getting completely away did wonders for Loren's outlook when he returned to the dirty business of war and revolution. He had been successful in arranging a series of meetings with Ramon Magsaysay and found that they had many ideas and concepts in common. Magsaysay, a former military officer, was tall for a Filipino and had a great deal of personal charisma. Loren found that he enjoyed working with him.

They spoke together in his office. "What I am looking for, Commander, is a more compact, faster reacting armed force to deal with the guerrillas in the hills."

"That's exactly what we need, Mr. Secretary. A way to hit them hard and fast before they can disappear into the jungle."

"I'm thinking of a completely new suite of arms to complement a fast moving strike force. There are those in the government who oppose this point of view."

"I'll see what I can do to get you some U.S. support on that issue, sir. I'll also look into what new military hardware from the U.S. would be appropriate."

"Splendid, Commander. Between the two of us, we might be able to make some good things happen." The two men shook hands.

As he worked with Magsaysay and the others, Loren thought about what they might do to stem the Huk tide. A germ of an idea was forming his mind that just might turn the tables on the communist inspired guerrillas, but it was too soon to discuss it. With some courage and daring, he thought, there was a way to get at them in their mountain strongholds. He resolved to bring it up with Pat when he returned to the U.S.

As the time to return to the U.S. came nearer, Loren concentrated on getting as much intelligence on the Huks as he could, both military and political. Magsaysay helped him significantly in this effort. "The enemy is now acknowledging their communist leadership openly," he told him. "They are broadcasting that they are organizing the Red Army of the Philippines to triumph for communism."

"Yes, I've seen some of those reports. There are also intelligence reports of violence in the countryside of Central Luzon. The Huks are trying to intimidate any of the local population who oppose them. They're in there in the villages making propaganda speeches and trying to gain peasant support."

Magsaysay shook his head. "It looks like a full-scale effort to take over."

The Huks had openly opposed the Bell Act, a proposed trade agreement with the U.S., but when a referendum on the issue was held, the population, most of which was urban, voted to pass the bill into law. Loren saw it as a confrontation between a business-oriented city population and the agrarian countryside rather than a contest between political ideologies. Nevertheless, as the split between the Huks and the Central government widened, it looked to him as though the nation was moving toward a major civil war.

The Government was holding a huge, outdoor political rally at the Luneta on a warm summer night in July. Excitement was in the air as many thousands crowded around the dais to hear the speeches. President Quirino himself gave an address extolling the democratic traditions of the Philippines and stressing the populace's duty to uphold these traditions in the upcoming elections. Ramon Magsaysay also addressed the throng about the measures they were taking against the attempted communist revolution.

Loren and Maria stood in the crowd listening. They were close enough to see the presenters quite clearly and the public address system was deafening. Loren had his arm around Maria's waist when the bomb exploded. He instinctively covered her as debris rained down on where they stood. Something sharp sliced through the back of his jacket, but amazingly did not draw any blood.

Loren looked at the carnage around them. Bloodstained people stumbled along, crying. Bodies lay strewn across the green grass. "We've got to get away from here!" He held Maria closely as he pushed his way through the panicking crowd. They reached their car and, with great difficulty, got through the jam of other vehicles. Loren held her close to him as they drove out to the villa. When they were upstairs, Loren slipped off his jacket to survey the damage. The metal shard had sliced neatly through the fabric, leaving an eight-inch tear in the material. Maria came to him, limping slightly.

"Are you hurt, Loren?"

"It looks like I was very lucky. Are you all right?"

"I just twisted my ankle a little when we were leaving the rally. Oh, Loren, that was terrible! I didn't think things like that could ever happen here."

"The Government is going to have to deal with those people, sooner or later! If they don't move soon, they're going to lose what control they have." Loren's voice had an edge as hatred coursed through him. If they had harmed Maria...! They held one another close in the night.

Loren had finished early that Friday at the Malacanang Palace and was back at the Manila Hotel at five that evening. His activities in the Philippines were finally winding down and he was starting to make plans for travel back to the U.S. He was looking forward to meeting Maria for dinner later that evening. He knew that he would miss her terribly when he had to return to Washington. He had just stepped out of the shower when his telephone rang. "Yes?"

"Loren, this is Tom Kite."

"Well, son of a gun, hello! I was hoping to hear from you, but I wasn't sure you were in Manila. Your boss was telling me that you were up country fighting guerrillas. Where are you?"

"I'm down here in the lobby. I thought you might want to tip one or two."

"Give me ten minutes. I'll meet you in the bar." He didn't see Tom immediately when he entered, until Tom stood up and waved. "It's great to see you, Tom! Tell me what you've been up to since we last heard from you."

"Well, as you said, mostly up country fighting guerrillas. Felice and I have an apartment here in Manila. We're going to be parents in about six months."

"Hey, that's wonderful. I'm glad everything's worked out for the two of you, but I'm sorry you're not with us back in the U.S."

"I like living here and we don't have the problems that you and I discussed once. Did you hear any more about our people on Mindanao?" Loren went on to tell him about the Japanese POW list. Tom shook his head. "But nothing about Ramon and Tomi?"

"I even had the Philippine Government looking for them, but we came up dry."

"I'm sorry to hear that." He paused. "I had another subject that I wanted to bring up, too."

"What's that?"

"People are starting to talk about you and Maria Castillejos. Felice told me that some of her friends knew about you and her."

Loren was silent for a moment. "I see. I guess we knew it was going to happen eventually. I remember not so long ago when you were telling me about your love for Felice. Now I'm telling you. I love her, Tom."

"Does any one know back in the states?"

"I don't think so."

"What are you going to do?"

"I don't know, Tom. I don't know."

Loren and Maria said their goodbyes at the villa the night before he was due to fly to the U.S.

"I wish you didn't have to go, Loren. I wish you could stay here with me."

"I have to go back, Maria. There are many things to do, things to help the Philippines. Will you be here for me when I return?"

"Yes, Loren, I will." They embraced one last time.

Loren began his long journey to Washington and Chevy Chase the following day.

CHAPTER XXIV—HOME AGAIN

Beverly was waiting for him when he came through the gate at National Airport. They had a happy reunion as they embraced in the busy terminal. In a half-hour, they were on their way to Chevy Chase.

Bev was talking as she drove. "You know, I haven't been here that long either. I just returned from Portland a little more than three weeks ago. It was sort of strange, coming back to the empty house."

"We'll have to throw a party or something. Sort of get back into the swing of things."

"Sounds good. Oh, Loren, I saw JoAnne when I was in Portland."

"You did? My God, how is she?"

"She has aged. I guess that's understandable."

"Yes. What else?"

"Well, she is still single and living at home with her dad and mom. She's seeing someone now. I met him. He seems like a nice person."

Loren was silent for a minute as he drove. Then he turned to look at Bev. "Is she…all right?"

"Yes, I think so."

The next few days were pleasant, getting to know each other again. They found that they really didn't want to be social just then.

Before they knew it, the CIA parties were getting underway as the holiday season approached.

At work, Loren plunged into the task of documenting all he had observed during the last few months, with recommendations for further actions. He spent all of his first morning with McFadden, covering just the highlights of his time in Manila. When they broke for lunch, Loren asked Pat for some more time to discuss an idea he had regarding the Philippine situation.

Pat checked his schedule. "I'm stuck in meetings for most of the afternoon. Why don't we get a conference room in the morning so you can tell me about your idea. Should we have anyone else there?"

"Not right now, Pat. I need to bounce this off you first."

"Let's do it. By the way, who is Maria?"

Loren swallowed hard. "You must mean Maria Castillejos. She's the daughter of one of the Philippine diplomats. Why?"

"Someone told me that they had seen you and someone by that name in one of the big nightclubs in Manila."

"We did a few things together. I played golf almost every weekend with her parents and her at their club."

"I see. Let me know where and when for tomorrow."

"Will do." As he walked back to his office, he wondered who had told Pat about Maria, and how much else he might know.

They met at nine the following day in one of the small conference rooms. Loren started with a summary of government campaigns against the Huks, all of which had been almost completely unsuccessful. "By the time they get there with their troops and ordnance, the Huks are far away. On this last trip, I had a chance to meet extensively with the Defense Secretary's deputy, Magsaysay. He wants to streamline the government units and organize them to be a fast reaction force. Small, heavily armed formations that can move to a designated spot in a hurry are what he's after. He feels that the Central Government will not give whole-hearted support on this. Is there anything we can do to make them listen?"

"I'll take that as an action item. Proceed."

"The problem is, with their broad base of peasant support, the Huks are always tipped off when government forces are on the move. Magsaysay can put together a fast reaction capability, but it won't help if the government forces don't know where the Huks are, especially the leaders."

"That seems to be the major problem. What do you propose to alleviate it?"

"I had this idea, no details yet, but we need to put some people up in those mountains covertly so that the peasantry doesn't know they are there. The mission would be to target Huk concentrations and leadership without their knowing it. Then hit them with close air support as well as Magsaysay's fast reaction forces. If we are successful, there shouldn't be many Huks left."

"That sounds like what we want to do all right, but how do you propose to insert your team without being observed?"

"I considered several ways, but the best I think would be a low level drop, say at nightfall up in the hills."

"I don't have to tell you how risky that might be. Nevertheless, I like your idea. Develop a full-fledged operational plan, and we'll present it to the powers that be. Make it your top priority, but keep it separate from your trip report. I don't think we want to set dates just yet. Kangleon and Magsaysay will need some time to reorganize their military forces. Also, with the Philippine elections coming up, the situation might change dramatically."

"Based on what I've seen, I wouldn't count on it. The Huks are winning, and they have no reason to try for a peaceful solution. I'll get started on the plan right away."

The CIA Ladies' Golf Association held their election of officers and Beverly was the new President. The installation dinner took place at a country club where they played regularly. The CIA purchased large blocks of time for its employees and official visitors at the picturesque course.

During the swearing in ceremony, Loren ran into Bob and Cara Lee. Bob and Loren shook hands. "Well, I see the traveler has finally returned! You were out there for a long time."

"Almost six months. A lot of things took place while I was there, most of them bad."

"That's what I understand. I have a copy of your report on my desk now. I haven't finished it yet, but it seemed like there was almost a career's worth of happenings."

Cara Lee was looking at him. "It's well that they brought you back when they did, Loren. Bob, have you noticed the onset of Asiatic features? A mandarin mustache would have been next."

"Very funny," Loren replied with a grin.

"Through it all, however, you still have that look we talked about before you left. Are there any canaries left at your house?"

"Not a one." Bev joined them then, and the conversation changed to golf.

Loren and Beverly were slowly working their way back into the local social scene, after having been gone so long. The members of the social committee organized an agency wide Halloween Party, and Loren came as Count Dracula with Bev as one of his "converts." Cara Lee, dressed like the local hostess for "Weird, Weird World," looked very sinister.

Loren sought to nibble on her neck later in the evening. "It's in the vampire tradition, Cara Lee," he said, winningly.

"In a pig's eye!"

Bob, in his warlock costume, had just finished dancing with Bev and was right beside them. "Uh...Bev, I don't have any whole blood to spare either." The four of them cracked up. The socializing was all in good fun and the event was a big success among the partygoers.

With the holidays close at hand, Bev had signed them up for a gourmet dinner exchange that involved several couples. She explained to Loren that the host couple was responsible for the main course, while the guests brought things like soups, salads and desserts.

"When is it our turn for the main course?"

"Next week."

"I'd like to do Pork Adobo. It's a traditional Philippine dish that I made a point of getting a recipe for."

"Sounds wonderful. The kitchen is all yours." The entrée was a big success.

Thanksgiving and Christmas was upon them. They decided to spend the holidays on the East Coast with his family, but Bev wanted to do something more. "How about Barbados?" Loren asked. "I've got a couple of weeks of vacation coming."

Bev put her arms around his neck. "That sounds heavenly, Loren."

The next two fabulous weeks, they played many rounds of golf in the bright sunlight of the Caribbean. In the warm tropical nights, they made love and both were relaxed and sated. The day before their scheduled departure, Loren and Beverly stretched out in their canvas chairs on the beach and sunned.

Bev touched his hand. "This has been so nice being away from everything and just being together." She paused for a moment. "I wanted you to know that you have a wife again, too."

"It's been nice, Bev."

"I had hoped that I might join you on one of your Philippine trips so that we could do something like this."

"You don't want to be over there now, Bev. The situation is really deteriorating. A bomb exploded at a big political rally in downtown Manila this summer. I was there. There were people killed and many injured. From the reports I've been receiving recently, things are getting worse."

"I didn't know."

"It's all going to come to a head very soon. There is a strong possibility that we won't be just observers. Please don't discuss that with anyone."

"I guess I'll have to be content with trips to Barbados."

"Do you think you can handle that?" Loren said with a grin.

After the holiday parties and their glorious vacation in the Caribbean, it was back to work with a vengeance for Loren. Upper management avidly read his lengthy report on conditions that he had observed in the Philippines and on events in which he had taken part. Loren increasingly participated in high level planning sessions for the CIA's role in the Philippines and Southeast Asia.

He resumed meeting with Carlos Romulo to establish a conduit with the Philippine Government. In the windowless conference room, Romulo talked to him about the current situation. "The Central Government is now fully supporting Kangleon and Magsaysay in their effort to streamline the Philippine Armed Forces."

"I'm glad to hear that this has finally come about. It could mean the difference when the time comes."

"On the negative side, the Huk presence is spreading still further. They have established themselves in the Sierra Madre Mountains in Southern Luzon, much closer to Manila. I don't have to tell you that the countryside is in turmoil."

"When the army completes their reorganization, we'll have to see what can be done about this."

"Yes, we will."

Loren had just sat down at his desk when the telephone rang. Pat was on the other end. "Have you heard?"

"About what?"

"Two major American publications with left leaning sympathies have just published exposes of corruption and graft in the Philippine Islands Government. I've got copies in my office if you want to see them."

"On my way."

Romulo called Loren when he became aware of the content and requested a meeting. Loren went to the embassy that afternoon. "How about it, Carlos. Is this really true or is it just journalistic sensationalism?"

"Please, Loren, not to go beyond these walls, but yes it is true. There was no law during the occupation and lawlessness has become a way of life after the war."

"There were rumors when I was in Manila this summer. I don't have to tell you how this might affect American public opinion. Is there anything that could be done at this late date?"

"I will send a report in the strongest words possible about what we have discussed. It is for President Quirino to take action."

"I have been tabbed to be an observer for the elections this summer. If there is anything I can do, please tell me."

"I will, Loren, and thank you."

His second martini tasted very good after the revelations of the day. Bev and he were to go to Bob and Cara Lee's for a gourmet club dinner that evening. Bev had prepared Pancit Molo, a Philippine version of won ton soup, from a recipe Loren had brought back. As he was sipping, he watched her prepare for the evening.

Bev, in her early thirties, was slender and trim as a model. With her radiant complexion, she looked like a young girl. She was a tremendous asset in his personal relationships with fellow workers and management. Always elegant, well-spoken, active in the CIA's social whirl, she was an ideal wife for him and his career. Only motherhood, though she was eminently suited for it, was not part of her life. They had talked again about adoption, but Bev seemed to shy away from the idea. Lately, she had been seeing another doctor for a second opinion on whether she could bear children. He hoped that she would decide on a course of action before they reached an age where parenthood would not be practical.

They had a pleasant evening out, enjoying the international cuisine with Bob, Cara Lee and three other couples. Loren's mind was miles away as he considered what was in his future as far as the Philippines. If all this takes place as planned, he would be going behind enemy lines again. Caught up in the excitement of it, he looked forward to what was coming. He thought of Maria and knew that he would have to make some lifetime decisions and soon. He made small talk with the others while he considered the future.

Pat McFadden held an inhouse review of Loren's covert action plan against the Huks. Several of Loren's peers participated. Afterwards, one of the attendees spoke up. "You know, the real problem with your scheme is the parachute jump. It takes a real expert to pull off a jump like that from that low an altitude."

"Not necessarily," returned Loren. "Not with the right people and the proper amount of training."

"That would have to happen. No one in this organization has ever made a parachute jump, at least not that I'm aware of."

"Like I said, with the right people, it can be done."

After a week of discussions and suggestions, Pat pronounced it ready for presentation to upper management.

With the completion of the review, Pat asked Loren to stop by his office. With the door closed, Pat discussed the mission's implementation with him. "Well, your plan survived pretty much intact from the original. One of the things I had a question on was the six-man team. You didn't define its composition."

"I want at least one Filipino and preferably more, and of course, I'll make the jump."

"How will you present the proposal?"

"I'll make the formal proposal of the action to the Colonel and Magsaysay and we'll tentatively schedule it for the fall after the elections."

"Loren, you will probably be chosen to head this mission if it is deemed necessary. This doesn't mean that you have to go behind enemy lines again. It might be best if you ran the show from the air base."

Loren was taken aback. "I never thought about not making the jump. I wouldn't know what to do if I were not on the ground with the team."

"Someone will have to coordinate with the army's quick deployment units to make sure that they have current and correct information. The air strikes will have to be coordinated so we don't blow up our own people. There are a hundred other details that you will have to deal with as they come up. Who is going to do that if you are in the jungle?"

"I know that these things are necessary for the success of the mission, but I hadn't thought of myself in that role."

"If you are the man in charge, you have to think about those things. I'm not sure that anyone else could do it. It's your decision, of course, but you should consider putting yourself down at least as a supernumerary for the actual show."

"I'll have to think about it, Pat. I know what you are saying, but I've just never considered that possibility."

Loren was amazed at how quickly the time passed, as he tried to keep up with the constantly changing situation in the Philippines, nine thousand miles away. Preparations for the elections were underway and hopes were high, though CIA management was concerned over the potential of Huk intimidation of rural voters. Other than occasional dinner parties, he and Beverly led a quiet existence. Washington was experiencing one of the worst winters in some years, and the ice and snow discouraged doing a lot of things.

Much to his surprise, Loren found Don Buchman waiting for him in his office when he came to work. "Son of a gun, it's been awhile. Hello, Don!" He knew that Don had been working for sometime in another of the Far East sections.

"Hello, Loren. A little birdie told me that you may be taking another hike in the jungle one of these days."

Loren gave him a surprised look. "Where did you hear that?"

"It's just a rumor that has been floating around. If there is any truth in it, keep me in mind."

"You know I can't discuss anything that might be in the works. However, if something does come up, I'll get on to you."

"Thanks a lot, Skipper. I've got to shove off now. Good talking to you again."

"My pleasure." Later that week, Loren took the first steps to obtain a transfer to his section for Buchman.

Loren was doing serious physical training, looking ahead to when he might be in the field again. He spent several days in weapons qualification on the CIA ranges and took a refresher course in hand-to-hand combat. Beverly watched all of these things happening but said nothing. In early May, Loren, Don Buchman and two others from his organization spent two weeks at Fort Bragg, in North Carolina. His cover story was a strategic planning meeting, but they were really there for parachute training.

Loren's first jump was an incredible experience for him. As the air streamed by the open door, he fixed his static line to the cable above his head and plunged headfirst into space. The jolt of his opening chute brought him up short and then he was floating down to the open area far below. He landed hard, but tumbled with the force, just as his jump instructor had told him. When he had disengaged from his billowing chute and was standing in the tall grass, his first feeling was one of exhilaration. He couldn't wait to do it again!

At the end of two weeks, they had made six jumps and each of them felt confident in his ability. They would undergo advanced low level jump training in the fall when he got back from the Philippines.

When Loren returned from Ft. Bragg, he found that Pat McFadden had set him up to present a briefing on his covert action plan, code-named Operation Hammer, to upper management. "This will be a formal briefing in the large conference room. Put on your bib and tucker and tell them all about it."

"I'm ready, Pat."

Dressed in his best Brooks Brothers suit, Loren presented his plan much as he had the original, in house. He described the operation clearly and concisely, and there were few questions. Two days later, Pat asked him to come to his office. "Well, you're going to lead the operation and brief it to the Philippine Government. Congratulations!"

"Thank you, Pat. I'll do what it takes to make it happen."

Afterwards, he felt gratified that his work gained approval so readily. In further discussions, CIA management decided that he should not brief the mission until after the election and then only if the Huk situation was threatening. Loren was content with this.

Beverly and Loren were enjoying a quiet evening together. Loren was talking about dining out and saying they should do it more often.

"I'm glad you mentioned dining out, Loren. Tell me, have you ever had Greek cuisine?"

"No, but I guess it's a lot like Armenian food, shish kebobs and all."

"I'd like to go to a Greek restaurant in downtown Washington this Saturday. Are you game?"

"Sure, but what's so special about this Saturday?"

"They have Greek dancing. I understand it's very good."

"OK, let's do it."

"I'll make the reservations."

They had enjoyed a delicious meal of shashlik and were sipping ouzo as the show started. The belly dancers were marvelous as they shook to the tambourines. They danced gracefully, belted just below their bare midriffs with coins, which chinked to the rhythm of the Greek instruments. The dancer in front was far more voluptuous than the other two, but all three were lovely. As he watched, he suddenly thought that his eyes were playing tricks on him. The dancer in front with the almost transparent veil was Cara Lee! Then the identity of the other two dancers registered as well.

"My God!" he managed to say. Bev was in hysterics. Loren looked for the husbands of the other two dancers who were fellow workers. As he spotted first one and then the other, he also saw Bob in a corner by the stage. Everyone was enjoying his reaction. When he recovered, he stood up from the table. "I feel like dancing too!"

Bev was tugging at his arm, trying to stop him, but she was too weak from laughter. He finally relented. In a few minutes, the dancers and their husbands joined them at their table.

"When did all of this happen?" asked Loren, unable to come up with anything else.

Cara Lee looked at him and smiled. "We've been practicing for three months and this is our debut. Our instructor is the headliner here." She paused for a moment. "We fooled you, didn't we?"

"That you did, Cara Lee, that you did." He ordered ouzo all around to celebrate.

CHAPTER XXV—HUK!

The Pan American Clipper flight touched down at Manila airport a little after nine. Two of the junior members of the diplomatic corps were there to meet Loren and expedite his way through customs. Every year, those who met him at the plane were younger, or maybe he was just getting older. His luggage disappeared into the waiting limousine and he was on his way again to the Manila Hotel.

He knew there were newer, more modern hotels in the city now, but all of Manila's activities still seemed to center on that venerable piece of real estate, now completely repaired from the war damage. When he checked in, he again found the familiar embossed envelope. He looked forward to an elegant dinner at the Castillejos' the following evening and to seeing his love again. Loren, in his eagerness, considered breaking the rules and calling Maria once he was in his room, but it was late. He decided that he should wait until tomorrow evening, knowing that he would think of her all through the day.

The picture presented at the Palace in his briefings the following day was bleak. The countryside north of Manila, deserted because of Huk terrorism, lay fallow. The farmers had quit farming and had crowded into the city for survival. Hunger was starting to become a problem in Manila.

Nevertheless, preparations for the elections were on track and the Central Government, the presenter maintained, had high hopes that they would receive a firm mandate to carry on. Loren was skeptical. The Huks had nothing to gain from the democratic process. He arranged to meet with Colonel Kangleon and Ramon Magsaysay the following day. The state of the military would determine what options were available against the Huks.

That evening, as Loren stepped outside through the hotel's main entrance, he saw that there was only a small cab rank in front. The streets close by, normally crowded with people who were on the town for the evening, were strangely deserted. Most unusual, he thought. The Manila doorman hailed him a cab and he was on his way to the Castillejos.

She was waiting for him, framed in the doorway of the library when he entered her house. He went quickly to her and then she was in his arms. Maria gave him a dazzling smile. "Close the door, Loren." He did as he was bid. Then they embraced happily. She looked at him with her soft brown eyes. "Loren, I have missed you so. I try to tell myself that you are like a sea captain who is away for long periods on a voyage. I only wait for the day when you are here again."

They embraced once more, and Loren felt suspended in time and space. "I love you, Maria."

They went in to meet the other guests with Maria on his arm. He shook hands warmly with Manuel Castillejos and greeted his wife and the other guests. As they dined, he looked at Maria, seated directly opposite him. Poised and elegant, she conversed with her guests. In the three years he had known her, she had gone from a lovely young girl to an accomplished, beautiful young woman. In a letter she had written to him some months ago, she had told him that she had completed her studies in Political Science at the University and was considering whether or not to do graduate level study.

After dinner, she told everyone that they were going to a party at one of her friends. As soon as they were away from the house, Maria drove directly to her aunt's villa.

Loren was surprised. "Is your aunt still away?

"Yes. They really like Paris. They have no plans to return right now."

"We should send her a thank you note."

Maria laughed. "Yes, we should." They walked up the broad stairway, hand in hand.

Maria, naked, was startlingly beautiful. Overcome by the sight and feel of her, he caressed her incredibly soft skin and full breasts, responsive to his touch. She had tiny, delicate features and shell-like ears, beautifully convoluted like sculpture. Her black shining hair fell to her loins. After being apart for so long, they loved with a special ardor.

Afterwards, as they lay side by side, her small hand in his, they talked. "How long will you be here, darling?"

"I'm not sure, but definitely through the elections and their aftermath. I am an official observer and there are other things to deal with as well. Do you want to go downtown tonight?"

"We can't, Loren, not any more. It's not safe on the streets. Huk gangs are everywhere!"

Loren once more felt the anger rise in him. If he had his way, there would be a day of reckoning, and soon. "I wondered about the deserted streets. The Government has to act, to do something!"

"But, what can they do? There has been fighting for over three years and the Huks are getting stronger."

Loren's eyes narrowed. "There are ways."

Election Day came and the Central Government was a clear winner, but then the rumors started. At the palace, Loren heard stories of stuffed ballot boxes in the city and ballots from the Huk dominated countryside being mysteriously lost. Protests raged in the newspapers and on the radio.

The Huks, broadcasting from their own propaganda stations, vowed retribution. "We have previously been militarily on the defensive against the aggression of the Central Government and have not committed to fight against the basic laws of the land," the broadcast intoned. "Now, because the Central Government has provoked us, we swear to overthrow the established order by violence!" The left wing newspapers railed against the "dirty elections" and blamed everything on the misuse of government power.

A somber group met at the Malacanang Palace after the announcement of the final election results. Loren had set up talks with

Colonel Kangleon and Ramon Magsaysay again to discuss their options against the Huks. They sat in a windowless room around a table, Loren, the Colonel and Magsaysay. Loren decided the time had come. "I've been authorized by my superiors to brief you on a proposed operation." The men in the room showed immediate interest.

Two hours later, the mood in the room had changed from dejection to jubilation. Magsaysay was ecstatic. "We can do it! We can put people up there to target the Huk positions. They will never know what hit them!"

Colonel Kangleon, in his chair at the head of the table, wore a serious expression. "Of course we can." He looked at Loren. "Who did you have in mind for your six man team, Commander?"

"Let's talk about it, Colonel." Loren requested the scout Carlos Delgado, who had been with him on his last Leyte mission, and one more Filipino from the younger recruits. "I'd also like to have Tom Kite."

"I was thinking of him, too."

"Don Buchman, whom I'm sure you remember, will also be part of the team. We'd like to include two of our new team members so that we can start to build a cadre for the future."

"That's six, Commander. What will your part be in the mission?"

"I will be coordinating the action from Clark AFB. I will also be the supernumerary if anyone gets hurt."

Magsaysay spoke up. "I have heard of your prowess, Commander. I would like to see you lead this. I would like to go with you."

"My boss says I should coordinate on this one. I know how you feel. The people we pick for this will have to do jump training in the U.S. and some other training as well. I will do full training with them, just in case. By the way, the code name for this mission is Operation Hammer."

They spent the next few days interviewing potential team members and ascertaining availability of those that they wanted. Tom Kite arrived later in the week to join their discussions. "Well, Skipper, it looks like we're going to do it one more time."

"One more time, Tom. If we do it right, we'll never have to do it again."

Maria lay close to him, curled up under his arm. "Why must you go back so soon, Loren? You've been here such a short while."

"This time I will be in Washington for only a little while and then I'll be coming back on a detail with the Department of National Defense for at least six months. I'll be training some people for specialized assignments with the Army. The bad thing about it is that I will be mostly at Clark Field and I won't be able to see you every day."

"If you are here, we'll find a way, Loren." He kissed her tenderly.

Loren hit the ground running on his return to Washington. He had another voluminous report to generate on the election and, at the same time, had to organize and schedule training for the selected team members of Operation Hammer.

In mid morning, Loren received a call that Tom Kite and two others were waiting for him in the lobby. He strode down the hall to the reception area. "Tom! It's good to see you back in the U.S.A. again."

"Good to be back, Skipper."

Then he saw another familiar face off to the side. "Carlos!" The two men shook hands. "It's been a long while."

"Just like the old days, Senor. This young guy here is Eduardo Bueno."

"It's good to meet you, Eduardo. If you all have badges from security, let's go down to my office where we can talk."

When they were all settled around Loren's desk, he continued. "First up, I've scheduled elementary jump training at Ft. Bragg for you. When you complete that, Carlos and Eduardo will take the covert mission training that the CIA regularly runs. Our whole team will be taking advanced low-level jump training at Bragg after the first of the year. On top of this, I've put together a rigorous physical training regimen for team members. We'll do the physical drill together whenever we have the chance so that everyone will be in peak condition for the second session at Bragg. Tom, while Carlos and

Eduardo are undergoing training, you and I will work together on the planning aspects of the mission. Any questions?" They were officially under way.

Bev had set up a dinner party with four other couples, including Bob and Cara Lee, as a sort of welcome home for Loren. The main topic of conversation was summer golf. In the course of the evening, Bob asked Loren about playing golf in the Philippines. "Not this year. Right now, it can be dangerous to get out on the course in the Islands."

"Really! I hadn't realized the situation had deteriorated that far. Are they going to be able to hold on over there?"

"We should know really soon, Bob. We are doing everything we can to shore up the Central Government, a lot of money, food, supplies, and particularly war materiel. Besides what you would normally expect, weapons and ammunition, we are even supplying armored vehicles."

"And people like yourself are counseling them on how to apply all of this."

"To a degree. We have several teams acting as advisors to the Philippine Government in matters like the economy, technology and even political issues, but what they do is ultimately their decision."

"Are you scheduled to go back again soon?" asked Cara Lee.

"I've been requested to do some guerrilla training for the Army starting in the spring."

"Do you know for how long?" She was looking at him in a way that made him wonder what she was thinking.

"I'm looking at six months."

"Poor Bev. She's going to be all alone again."

"It can't be helped."

Bob asked about his latest report. "It will be distributed in the next week or two when everyone signs off. It's not very encouraging reading."

"So I understand."

After the guests had left, Beverly talked to him. "Loren, is there something going on that I don't know about? Cara Lee is acting kind of funny."

189

"There's a great deal going on right now, Bev. As for Cara Lee, I can't speak for her."

The Philippine team went home for the holidays and, finally, Loren had a little time to catch up on being home again. He promised they would visit her parents for the holidays that year, so they flew to Portland in the third week of December. Surrounded by family and friends, Beverly was the center of attention, while Loren stayed mostly in the background. He was affable and pleasant when it was necessary, but mostly he could disengage.

Beverly's father attempted to draw him out regarding his work but, of course, there was very little Loren could tell him. Her father was a relatively small man physically, and it was apparent from the fit of his clothes that he was living a life of ease and plenty. One morning when Loren was shaving, Reverend Jones passed by him in the hall. He stopped short and almost gasped. "What is that scar on your shoulder, Loren?"

"Hasn't Bev told you about this?"

"No, no she hasn't."

Loren was imposing physically and the Reverend Jones continued to stare. "I was wounded on a mission in the Philippines. A firefight with a Jap patrol. Bev insisted that I go to the hospital with her. She applied sulfa to the wound and put new dressings on it daily. I'm afraid she babied me a lot," he said, smiling.

The Reverend Jones laughed. "Well, I'm glad to see she got you home in one piece."

The high point of the trip for Loren was a motor trip up to Timberline Lodge on Mt. Hood. The snow was falling heavily and the ethereal beauty of the mountain was something to behold. He put his arm around Bev as they watched the huge flakes floating down. For a short while, all of life's problems and difficulties seemed to disappear as they absorbed the majesty of this wonder of nature.

The days passed quickly and soon it was time for them to return. Bev's family drove them to the airport and wished them well as they said their goodbyes. Then Bev and Loren were on their way home to Washington.

In the third week of January, the whole team went to Ft. Bragg for three strenuous weeks of advanced parachute training. At the end, they were jumping at an altitude of four hundred feet. Loren was amazed at how quickly they were on the ground in this scenario. He also noted how small the margin for error was. Tom Kite injured his ankle on the last day, but it didn't appear to be serious.

When Loren returned, he had three weeks before he was due to go back to the Philippines. He was glad that the frenetic activity that had been part of his life since he returned from the Philippines was finally starting to taper off.

Beverly said that she was happy to have him back in the world again. "You've seemed to be preoccupied for a long time. It's nice to have you back, even though it's just for a little while."

"I'm sorry, Bev. As I told you, there is a lot going on right now. I've been up to my ears in work, and it's not going to slack off for some time yet."

"There's something big about to happen, isn't there?"

"You know I can't say anything, Bev."

"Yes."

Loren awoke refreshed after his long trip from the States. Pan American was flying DC-6s now and their higher performance shortened the flying time required, but it was still a very long haul from San Francisco. He was due at the Palace in a little over an hour when he stepped into the shower.

Senior military were everywhere when he walked through the main entrance. He had scheduled a meeting with the top echelon of the Defense Department in a secure conference room. With the government representatives seated around a large table, Loren called the meeting to order. He gave a report on the status of training for Operation Hammer and then discussed the schedule. After they finished, they selected a tentative date for the mission. Loren looked for Tom Kite, but he was not there.

He enumerated the milestones leading up to the operation and then addressed the company. "The first event on the schedule is the establishment of the MATS flight. This flight will begin, as soon as possible, to fly over the western mountains to Taiwan every evening at about 1700. We want the time to coincide with the time of last light

191

on the mission jumpoff date. The flight will pass over the projected jump zone at a low altitude. After a month or two, the Huks will grow accustomed to the aircraft's passage and, on D Day, we will parachute from four hundred feet."

They went on to discuss schedule issues for the rest of the morning. Loren spent the afternoon meeting with Magsaysay's contingent, discussing the state of the new streamlined motorized units in detail. He was impressed with the job the Filipinos had done in the reorganization of their ground forces. The new units were very mobile and well armed. The U.S. equipment and the tactics they had developed would allow them to hit swiftly and hard. The various pieces of the operation were starting to come together.

Late in the afternoon, Tom Kite came into the room where they were meeting. Much to Loren's astonishment, he was on crutches! "It's the ankle, Skipper. It was hurt worse than we thought back stateside. Now I'm having a problem getting it to heal properly."

With a rush, Loren thought what this meant. He would jump with his "stick" when the time came and operate, once more, behind the lines. "We've got it covered, Tom. I will go in your place. However, you are going to have to learn my job now. Are you game?"

"I'll do whatever is needed."

"Are you stationed at Basa Air Force Base now?"

"That's my jumping off point."

"We're going to have to spend a lot of time together for awhile. I'll arrange for some quarters there so we can meet when I'm done with the guerrilla training."

"Roger, Skipper."

Loren and Maria walked on the terrace at the Castillejos' before dinner. He had gotten away early and Maria greeted him at the door with joy. She clung to his arm as they walked. "Loren, I've been invited to spend some time with my friend, Alicia Ruidoso, at her family's country estate. It is quite close to Clark Air Force Base."

Loren smiled. "As you said, we will find a way. I'm going to be splitting time between Clark and Basa Air Force Base, so it looks like we can see each other when you are there. How long will your visit be?"

"As long as you are here." Loren kissed her hair as they walked.

Loren's rough and tumble guerrilla training classes saw him rise to a peak of fitness that he had not seen since the jungle days. They ran everywhere and the training exercises were very physical. When he was not on the training course, he spent time closeted with Tom Kite, going over the big picture for Operation Hammer and telling Tom what his duties in coordinating the operation would be. Tom was walking with a cane now, but was still not very mobile. Loren noted with satisfaction that the C-47 Skytrain was making its run to Taiwan every night at dusk. He reflected that the time was drawing near when the American team members would be flying in on MATS to start their on site mission preparedness.

Maria waited for him in the brown convertible at the end of the day. They would go into town for dinner and sometimes dancing every evening. They were a striking couple and heads would turn when they would enter. Afterwards, they would return to his quarters on the base to be together. On their first night, they talked in the dark. "My parents asked if I would be seeing you when I was here."

"Oh?"

"I think they wanted to ask about us, but they didn't. When this is all over, we need to tell them, darling."

"Yes."

Maria would leave early enough so that she was back at the Ruidoso's by ten. He worried about her driving alone, but the area around the military installations was populous, with busy traffic. On a regular basis, he was a guest of the Ruidoso's for dinner at their spacious country estate, just north of the base. Maria's friend Alicia was a beauty in her own right and many young men, some in uniform, joined them at the Ruidoso's. One evening, Alicia's guest was one of Loren's trainees.

Spring moved into summer and, one day, the MATS flight from the U.S. brought the American team members to the Philippines. Loren met them as they deplaned.

He shook hands with Don Buchman and the two new members that he had trained in the States, Lon Casey and Bill

193

Salkeld. "Welcome, gentlemen. We will have a team meeting tomorrow after you settle in. We have a lot to go over."

They met in a windowless conference room in a secure area the following day. Loren addressed the company. "We've had a roster change. Tom Kite has a bad ankle, so I will be taking his place as lead. Tom is learning my job as the overall effort coordinator. He will be scheduling air and ground strikes based on our input.

"Starting tomorrow, we will be training together. I am running guerrilla training for the Filipinos, so I will not be here all of the time. Our regimen will be mostly physical, like what we were following stateside. Don Buchman will coordinate this. There will be a team meeting here once a day to disseminate information and discuss our progress. The local situation is getting worse and it is close to true revolution, so time is important. The Huks have literally split the republic.

"Keep in mind that half of the twenty-one million population is here on Luzon, in Manila and north of us in the Huk dominated region. If the issue is resolved favorably here, we will have won the fight. When we think we are ready, I'll ask the Defense Secretary for a date. Right now, we are looking at sometime in September." A general murmuring took place as what he had said sunk in. "Before we adjourn, a word about outside the gate, especially for those who have not been in Asia before. Lon, Bill, I believe that applies to you."

"That's right sir," Lon answered. Slender and boyish, he was the more voluble of the two. Bill, solidly built and stolid, just smiled and nodded.

"Angeles, out there, is not Main Street, U.S.A. Some people go a little crazy when they first get here. Stay sober and just be cool. If you have to, use your cover story about training. We're going to be here a while and I don't want to lose anyone."

"Do you mean that some exotic female might try to compromise me in order to find out what I know?" asked Lon, hopefully. Laughter filled the room.

"You should be so lucky," returned Loren. "I'll see you tomorrow at the same time." The team members went away with a lot to think about.

A system of code words identifying grid positions and locations within a grid square was developed by American and Filipino cartographers. Loren explained to the combat team how the code word system worked with a three-dimensional model of the operations area that had been put together for the mission. It was extremely useful to the team in understanding the topography they would be infiltrating.

"There's a code word to tell the men on the ground that the Huks were pursuing them," Loren told them. "The people at Clark will monitor Huk communications for the entire mission to determine this." He hammered home one particular point. "If you are discovered, you must eliminate the people who have spotted you. Allow no one to get away. If anyone does, the whole Huk army will be out after you. Your best chance of success and survival is if no one knows you are there."

The team ran combat formations over rugged terrain and fired their weaponry on the ranges. Loren thought that the team's state of readiness was impressive. As their projected date grew closer, they were tuning to a fine edge.

The evenings with Maria were like a tonic to him. The hard training they were undergoing left him tired at the end of the day, but with her, the tiredness would evaporate in seconds. He was not looking forward to when the mission would require all of his time. He was due to attend a conference at the Malacanang Palace at the first of the week, where he expected to get at least a time window for their operation.

He spoke to Maria that night, giving her his cover story for his training mission. "Darling, we are going to be starting twenty-four-hour training exercises next week and then my detail here will be concluded. I think it would be better if you return home to your parents now, and I will see you in Manila when we are done."

"I knew it would be happening soon. Would you drive down with me this weekend?"

"I will."

The day was bright and sunny as they drove down to the city. They allowed plenty of time, because there was the possibility of delays at checkpoints on the way. Philippine armed forces personnel along with the police were searching vehicles for weapons coming into the city. A six o'clock curfew for traffic in and out of Manila was in force.

The Army stopped them twice at roadblocks and they found themselves stuck in endless lines of vehicles. Despite their early departure, it was dinnertime when they reached the center of Manila. As they drove through the streets, Loren saw many apparently destitute people. "Look at that, Maria. It's lots worse than when I arrived. That was only a few months ago."

"I know. It's terrible. Loren, it's getting late. Why don't we stop for dinner?"

"All right. Where would you like to go?" They decided to stop at a restaurant on Adriatico Street that they had frequented. There were few customers there as they enjoyed the haute cuisine.

Loren and Maria emerged from the restaurant to find men on both sides of the walk that led to their car. As they continued on, one of the men stepped in front of them. He held a knife in his hand. In a fraction of a second, Loren lashed out with his foot against the man's knee. The man fell screaming to the pavement, clutching his shattered leg. Loren felt a glancing blow to the back of his shoulder. He turned quickly and drove the heel of his hand under the other man's nose. The man went down without a sound and didn't move. The others scrambled back with eyes wide, then turned and ran. The whole thing was over in seconds.

Maria, terrified, clung to him. "Are you hurt, Loren?"

"No. Are you all right?"

"Yes."

"We need to get out of here now!"

They rushed to their car and drove rapidly away. When they arrived at the Castillejos' home, Maria, still badly shaken, sat silently in the living room. Loren talked to her father about what had happened. "There are two of them that won't be bothering anyone soon. One of them may be dead." Manuel Castillejos' eyes grew large. "Manuel, do you think I should inform the police?"

"Did anyone other than the assailants see you?"

"I don't think so."

"Let it be for now. I will make inquiries."

"Thank you, Manuel."

Loren entered a hotbed of political intrigue at the Malacanang Palace. The Colonel was at odds with the President and his staff again and threatening to resign. Rumors were rampant that Magsaysay would succeed him.

They were waiting to start their operations meeting when Carlos Romulo entered the room. Loren went to shake his hand. "Carlos, what brings you to Manila? I thought you were still back in Washington."

"You haven't heard then. President Quirino has appointed me as Secretary for Foreign Affairs in his government. We are still in the process of getting moved back to Manila."

"Well, congratulations. I'll be looking forward to seeing you while I am here."

When the Defense Department meeting began, the Colonel was not there. Magsaysay chaired it and started with a speech of welcome. "Colonel Kangleon is busy elsewhere today and won't be joining us. I'd like to welcome the Army and Air Force representatives of the Philippine Armed Forces who are with us today. I would also like to welcome Colonel Edward Lansdale of the U. S. Air Force who is here to consult with us on this operation."

Loren took note of the older officer who was his opposite number from OPC. Colonel Lansdale's specialty was psychological warfare, and he had developed a close personal relationship with Magsaysay. Loren had not met Colonel Lansdale before and made a mental note to spend some time with him while they were there.

Magsaysay turned to Loren. "And now I would like to turn this meeting over to Commander Loren Middleton who is in charge of this operation. Commander Middleton."

"Thank you, Mr. Magsaysay. The purpose of this meeting is to ascertain that all elements of the operation are in readiness. I've previously met with army and air force personnel while I was at Clark and I'm satisfied that they are ready to perform their part. A counterguerrilla force, a specially trained quick response unit, stands ready to close on the transmitted positions. Airborne rocket attacks, launched simultaneously from Clark and Basa Air Bases, will lead the way. All that remains is to set a date."

Discussions regarding the operation ranged over many subjects in the next few hours. When they at last finished, Magsaysay took the floor. "The operation will commence the day after tomorrow. All elements will hold themselves at the ready. When all last minute details are covered, we will transmit a single code word for final activation of Hammer. Let's make that word 'Tong'. Commander Middleton will insert his force that evening. Good luck to all of you!"

Loren returned to Clark in a staff car. As he rode back to the base, he could hardly contain his feelings of anticipation. At the team meeting the following morning, he delivered the final instructions. "We're all done training now. Our next action will be the real thing. Are there any questions?"

The men trooped out of the room to make their final preparations. Later in the day, they learned that Ramon Magsaysay had succeeded Colonel Kangleon as Secretary of the Department of National Defense. That night Loren could not sleep because his mind was racing through all the things they had to do.

The following afternoon, the combat team quietly replaced the airmen who had been loading the dummy cargo for Taiwan. Their radio equipment and ordnance went aboard in an innocuous shipping crate. Another crate contained their parachutes and camouflage gear. When the time for the flight came, another crew closed the cargo doors with Loren's team members inside. They quickly changed out of the air force work dungarees into their combat uniforms and stored their weapons and radio equipment for the jump. They had just finished when the port engine of the C-47 turned over. They were only minutes away!

CHAPTER XXVI—THE COVERT MISSION

The C-47 rolled down the taxiway and then turned onto the North/South runway. Loren heard the engines rev up, and then they were accelerating down the runway. The cargo aircraft cleared the runway boundary and then circled back around to a slightly north-of-west heading. The aircraft climbed slowly and was quite close to the mountain summits as it passed over them. A crewman popped the cargo door and the team stood up and fastened their static lines.

Here we go, thought Loren. The air rushing by the open cargo door almost drowned out the engine noise. The spotter in the copilot's seat saw the high meadow that was their drop zone. The jump indicator flashed green and, at last light, the team leapt into the semidarkness.

Loren's chute opened and within seconds, he was on the ground. He tumbled with the contact and then jumped up to reel in the billowing chute. Out of the corner of his eye, he saw two more chutes coming down. He ran for the edge of the jungle, carrying the awkward bundle. He blew the high-pitched whistle that was a signal to form up on him, and he saw the other five team members moving toward him with their chutes. According to their most recent intelligence, there were no Huks in their drop zone, but the team needed to get out of sight as soon as possible, just in case. He thanked God that there were no injuries.

"Bury the chutes back in the jungle. Make sure you cover up the fresh soil with some of the greenery." The team broke out their entrenching tools. When they finished, Bill Salkeld, who had the responsibility for communications, checked out the lightweight portable radio. In the black, tropical night, they unlimbered their automatic weapons and started climbing toward the summit of the ridge.

They had dropped on the far side of the mountains but were only a short distance from the ridge, where they would move down into the jungle greenery that contained the Huk forces. After they performed a quick reconnaissance of the area, Loren called the team together. "We're going to have to use the trails. If we try to cut our way through this underbrush, they will hear us coming for miles. We'll have to take our chances as far as running into night patrols. The Huks don't know that we're here, so we have the advantage. Let's head out." Two hours later, they entered the Huk sanctuary.

The team descended about five hundred feet and then Loren called a halt. "Don, you and Casey reconnoiter to the north." They prepared to shove off. "Carlos, you and Eduardo head down the mountain range to the south. See what Huk formations are in the area around us. Make sure all of you get back before daylight." The two Filipinos headed out. Loren stayed at the focal point with Salkeld and the communication gear, hidden in the dense jungle. He sent a prearranged code word out into the ether, indicating that they were in place, and received an acknowledge immediately. Now, all they had to do was find the enemy.

Buchman and Casey were the first to get back. Don reported what they had found. "There's a large Huk camp about five miles to the north. We went some distance beyond that but didn't find any evidence of more guerrillas in the area." Loren and Don huddled over their map grid and tentatively identified the location.

Sometime later, Carlos and Eduardo returned. Carlos talked to Loren. "There are two large encampments to the south, at about five miles and eight miles down the trail. We didn't go beyond the second camp." When they had identified the approximate locations of the southern encampments on the map, they saw the first gray traces of dawn on the horizon.

Loren looked around them. "Let's find a place to lay low for the day. There should be some places close to the trail we came down." Single file, they retreated into the jungle and, a short time later, found a level area overlooking the valley below. "They can't see us from the main trail. Let's get some rest." They settled down to wait for the following night. So far, Loren thought, it appeared that they had infiltrated the area without anyone knowing they were there.

Loren stood the initial watch, so it was near noon before he awoke to the bright, sunny day. After they had eaten their cold rations, he scanned the terrain below them in minute detail. He saw no sign of habitation. Don looked at him questioningly. "It looks like the army has staged away from the potential battleground. Let's get the rest of the team together to plan tonight's mission." They spent the next hour deciding on routes and what types of information to be collected. After reviewing the overall mission, Loren decided to leave the focal point of their operations at their current encampment for the present.

Loren talked to the team. "The largest concentration of Huks, and the one most likely to have a concentration of senior leadership, is the first camp to the south of us. We're going to have a real good look at them tonight. We'll use the whole team for a full reconnaissance of the position. Don, I want you and Carlos to find yourselves a good vantage point to observe the camp with your glasses during the day. We need to try to identify any senior leaders that might be there. We'll pick you up on the way south tomorrow night."

The team left their hiding place that evening, heading south to the guerrilla camp. With Don Buchman as the immediate focal point, Loren and the other team members infiltrated the jungle around the Huks. About three hours later, the first team member returned to the point. Loren and Eduardo were there fifteen minutes later. Within the next thirty minutes, all had returned. They held a brief conference, exchanging information on what they had observed. Buchman and Carlos Delgado prepared to stay behind to see if they could identify some of the Huk leaders. Loren talked to them. "You know what to do. After all the time we've spent looking at photographs, we should be able to do this without any problems. If there is any questions, check the photographs in your packs. Good luck, you guys."

"Good luck to you." Don and Carlos disappeared into the jungle. The rest of the team trudged silently down the trail to their original camp. A careful examination of the site revealed no evidence that anyone had discovered them. Loren reflected that they were really running in luck.

He generated a series of code words based on their activities that night and Salkeld transmitted them in a burst. Their message was acked immediately. Then they slept. The team would go to the Huk encampment farthest to the south the following night, according to plan. They would pick up Don and Carlos on the way. Loren stretched out on the ground. He looked at Bueno, who had the first watch, and the others, who were sleeping. We need to send a two-man team further south to look for more Huks, he decided. That means another place to stay tomorrow night. He stared at the starry sky above for several minutes before he finally drifted off to sleep.

The four men slipped by the large Huk camp that they had infiltrated the previous night, passing between the camp itself and the picket lines of guards lower down on the mountain. Using a jungle trail, they moved rapidly, avoiding Huk patrols. Again their luck held and they were into the empty jungle to the south. At a prearranged meeting point, Don and Carlos rejoined them.

They talked in a whisper. "We identified at least five Huk leaders from their photographs. There were a couple of others that we weren't sure of."

"What about Turac?"

"We didn't see him." Disappointed that they hadn't found the head man, Loren led down the jungle trail. They found the second Huk stronghold in the early hours of the morning. After searching for the better part of an hour, they decided on a hiding place above the camp. Overgrown with vegetation, it offered a good view of the camp and the surrounding area.

Loren called them together. "It's about four hours till first light. Lon and I are going to head south and see if we can find any more Huks. Don, set up at least a preliminary recon of this camp. We'll send what we have on the radio tomorrow."

He and Casey moved quickly down the trail in the pitch-black darkness. They were on their way a little over an hour when Loren raised his hand to halt. After a moment, Casey moved up next to him. Loren gave him his field glasses and pointed ahead. "Have a look."

Casey spent moments searching across their field of vision. "It's smaller than the other camps, but there are still a lot of guerrillas."

"Let's get closer." Beyond the camp, they could see the lights of Angeles and, on the horizon, Manila. The Huks were really close! "Lon, the range pretty much peters out beyond here. These are probably all the guerrillas we're going to find tonight. Let's get down to where they are and get as much data as we can. Do you think you can find your way back to this spot if we split up?"

"No problem, sir. How long should we take?"

"Let's make it an hour." They checked their watches and Lon disappeared into the darkness toward the far side of the camp. Loren followed, angling toward the near side. In twenty minutes, he was close to the periphery of the camp. He looked at the informal bivouac and thought how difficult it was going to be to get a troop count. They apparently had only small arms, with no artillery or armored vehicles in sight. Loren observed from three vantage points and then headed back to the rendezvous. He found Casey waiting for him. They spent a few minutes comparing what they had seen.

Loren glanced at the horizon. "We need to get back on the road. It's going to be daylight very shortly."

"Roger, Skipper." Loren thought that Casey must have heard some of the veterans address him that way. They got back to their hiding place with just minutes to spare.

Loren generated what had become a lengthy message, with all of the information they had accumulated in the last twenty-four hours. The burst mode of the transmitter kept the send interval short. They were acked immediately once more.

Loren spoke to his communications man. "Bill, how would you like to go with me down this hill a ways to get a look at the leadership in this camp?"

"Be with you in a minute." The two of them moved stealthily down the steep slope. They found an observation point that was within a hundred yards of the camp periphery. With their camouflage gear and face paint, they blended into the greenery. For three hours, they silently observed through their field glasses and made notes on potential IDs. Satisfied that they had thoroughly observed the camp, Loren signaled to Salkeld that they should withdraw. Climbing the steep slope to their hiding place was time consuming, because they were mostly crawling, close to the earth. They compared their IDs with pictures of the Huk leadership, and Loren coded and generated an additional message containing the agreed to information. Back at Clark, they had assigned code words to each of the photographs they had studied, so it was a relatively simple matter.

Afterwards, Loren talked to the team about their operation so far. "We are going to be stretching our luck to stay out here much longer. We need to do a thorough reconnaissance on the camp up north and then we should head up over the ridge. We'll send a 'go' to the Army and Air Force at that time." That night the whole team headed toward the north.

When day broke, they were off the trail in dense jungle, just below the northernmost camp. They had had a tension filled night as they bypassed the other Huk camps. They had narrowly avoided discovery by an enemy patrol near the largest one and now they were resting from their long hike.

Loren spoke to the team. "We need to try to ID some of the people here, but we can't get a look at the camp from where we are. We're probably not going to find a good vantage point until tonight."

Don got to his feet. "I'll go see what I can find."

"It's too dangerous in broad daylight when you don't know exactly where you are going, Don. We'll do our reconnaissance tonight and see what it looks like for tomorrow." The team slept fitfully, as the tension grew. At dark, with Buchman at the focal point again, the team spread out to view the camp from multiple vantage points. Moving silently, Loren avoided the guards and crept close to the encampment. He could hear them conversing from where he was. They spoke of a guerrilla action inside Manila. After he had listened for about a half-hour, he withdrew slowly and very quietly again. He took care not to disturb even the smallest twig. Three hours later, the team members were all back at the point. In the exchange of information, Loren whispered what he had heard.

"You heard them talking about this?" asked Buchman. "Did you have a cup of coffee too?"

Loren looked at him with a tired smile. "No, Don. I wasn't that close."

They moved silently down the trail to their hiding place. Loren, in the lead, heard footsteps coming. As they dove for cover, shots rang out. The patrol had spotted them!

The next few seconds were a maelstrom of fire. Loren emptied his magazine in the direction of the gun flashes he had seen. As he was changing his magazine, the team poured fire down the trail. They heard a scream of pain. A figure dashed across an open spot. Loren fired again and the man went down.

He leapt to his feet and motioned to the others. "Let's go!" He moved forward in a crouch, looking to either side. The others followed in combat formation. Suddenly they were in the middle of the Huk patrol. A bayonet came at him and Loren fired point blank. The force of the burst knocked the man back and he fell to the ground. The firing continued all around him and then, suddenly, there was silence.

He looked rapidly around the area. "Did we get them all?"

Don was by his side. "I think so, Skipper." They saw movement at the side of the road and everyone fired simultaneously. A man screamed and fell. Then, once more, silence.

Loren peered into the darkness. "Check the surrounding area! We can't afford to let anyone escape!" In the next few minutes, they made sure that no one was hiding closeby. They all stopped to listen, but there was no sound of movement.

Bill Salkeld called out as the attention light on the radio flashed. Bill listened momentarily, then turned toward them. "That's the signal that the Huks are looking for us."

Don nodded. "They heard the gunfire."

They moved rapidly on to their hiding place. Loren hurriedly coded the message describing their night reconnaissance. "Send this off as quickly as you can, Bill."

While Salkeld was sending, the rest of the team waited tensely, arms at the ready. Loren thought about what to do. He decided that they had only one choice.

He spoke quietly to the team. "We have to get off this trail right now. They'll be coming at us from both directions. We've got to climb straight up to the ridge." He checked his watch. "In thirty minutes, we'll send a 'go' for all four sites. We have about two hours until sunrise, so let's move."

They scrambled up the steep hill in the blackness. In their haste, they dislodged some small rocks that rattled on down below, but there was no response.

"Try to move more quietly," Loren whispered. "They'll see where we've gone soon enough!"

A half-hour later they halted and Salkeld sent the "go" to start the attack. Less than an hour later, as they climbed the steep terrain, Loren heard the sound of aircraft engines warming up.

They found some sparse cover high up on the mountain at the base of a large volcanic rock outcropping. Loren checked a potential route up to the summit with his field glasses. Going that way is going to be difficult, he thought. As the gray light turned into dawn, a large number of aircraft were rising from both Clark and Basa. Loren identified them as Corsairs, each with rockets mounted under their wings. After a few minutes, they formed up and wheeled toward the mountains.

Loren watched them come on. "Here we go. I hope those guys shoot good and straight."

The next thirty minutes were incredible. The team looked on as the mountain erupted repeatedly with terrific explosions. The Corsairs passed directly over them less than fifty feet above the terrain after they had launched their rockets. Then, through his glasses, Loren saw armored troop carriers on the valley floor.

"This is going to be a hell of a show," he mused. He scanned back down the trail that they had come up. A column of troops was climbing toward them! He was on his feet immediately. "The Huks are coming up after us. We've got to get out of here, now!"

The men scrambled to pack up their gear and Loren led off on the steep climb. They had been climbing for about an hour when the sounds of heavy ground fire and pitched battle reached them. He scanned down the trail again but there was no sign of their pursuers. Possibly, they were behind some mountainous terrain that hid them from view. Although it was broad daylight, they had to press on.

A steep traverse led to the saddleback above them. They couldn't see from where they were, but it was a good bet that the western slope of the range was immediately beyond. They climbed hand over hand up the nearly vertical slope. They were about fifty feet from the top when a piece of volcanic rock that Lon Casey was gripping broke away. He plunged down the slope, landing with a sickening thud. More than a half-hour later, they finally reached him.

As Carlos examined Casey for injury, Loren once more scanned the slopes with his glasses. He could see no cover of any kind where they were and he felt terribly exposed. However, he saw no sign of pursuing Huks.

Carlos came to him. "He has injured his shoulder. It is probably broken. He is only semiconscious now, but he should be OK."

"Can you rig a sling to protect the shoulder? We can probably carry him to the top, but it's not going to be easy." Loren ordered skirmishers out at fifty yards. If attacked, they had little choice but to fire from the prone position. He faced the problem of getting Casey up the last pitch of rock.

Lon was up on his feet, but was still a little woozy. Loren touched his good shoulder. "If we can form sort of a human chain, we can pass you up to the top. How do you feel? Can you help us by using your feet?"

"I think so."

"We've got to get moving right away." They fashioned a sling around Casey's waist that one of them could grip. "Be careful of that slag rock," he called out to the others. "It's not very solid."

Almost an hour later, they pulled Casey up to the summit of the ridge. The rest of the team lay on the ground at the top, exhausted. Once more, Loren scanned the terrain below them and found no pursuing troops. The din of battle below was general now. The sound of artillery and mortars punctuated the reports of many small arms. Their pursuers had apparently gone back when the shooting started.

Loren noticed a line of trees below them and to the left. No trails were visible through the scrubby undergrowth. He turned to the others. "There's nobody behind us anymore. Let's get down to those trees and get some rest. Bill, we need to send a message that we are on our way to the pickup point and schedule them for...tomorrow just before sunset."

Salkeld coded and transmitted the message. Loren spotted a stream bed leading to the west. "We'll follow that stream bed until we pick up a trail and then head for the ocean." He looked about him with an immense feeling of satisfaction. They were home free.

The cutter arrived on schedule at the inlet below the fishing village that was their pickup point. Loren and his team had to wade in deep water to get to it. The sailors pulled them aboard and then, wrapped in blankets, they rested as the cutter headed for the naval base on Subic Bay.

Don looked at him as they huddled on the deck. "We really clobbered them, Skipper." The others murmured agreement.

Loren raised his head wearily. "That we did."

A truck was waiting for them and they sped through the night to Clark Air Force Base. As the adrenaline drained from his body, Loren realized how exhausted he was. When the driver dropped him at his quarters, he immediately fell into the waiting bed.

Loren awoke to bright sunlight filtering through the blinds in his quarters. He checked his watch, on the nightstand, and was surprised to find he had slept for twelve hours. Refreshed, he plunged into the shower and then dressed in time for lunch at the Officer's Mess. Someone had left him a written message telling him about a 1500 debriefing. He had time to go back to his quarters and call Maria. One of the servants had answered the phone, and in a minute or two, he heard her voice.

"Maria, we're starting to wind down our exercises here at Clark. I'm planning on getting back to the hotel either late tonight or early tomorrow morning."

"Can you come to dinner tomorrow night? My parents have sent you an invitation to the hotel."

"That sounds marvelous. It looks like we're going to be busy all day at the Palace tomorrow. I miss you, and I'm looking forward to tomorrow night."

"So am I, darling. I wish you were here now, but I guess it will keep till then." They said their goodbyes and then Loren was due at the debrief.

When he entered the Malacanang Palace the next day, he noticed after a minute or so that people seemed to be looking at him as he passed. He had gotten a message telling him they were not going to start until eleven o'clock, which was something of a surprise. Loren headed to the main conference room. As he entered the room, the large number of people there all spontaneously stood and applauded. His surprise was complete.

Everyone who had a part in the operations in the mountains was there and caterers immediately laid on an elegant lunch. A bartender in the corner was mixing cocktails. They all seemed to have questions about the operation. Loren received many congratulations and slaps on the back as the team surrounded him. When he had sufficiently recovered, he rose to his feet and tapped on his water glass. "I want to thank all of you for your part in Operation Hammer. It couldn't have been done any better. Thanks again!" He waved to the crowd, to more applause.

Loren was talking with Tom Kite when the door to the conference room opened. Ramon Magsaysay came in to the room and went to shake Loren's hand. "Outstanding, Commander! They never knew what hit them!"

"Thank you. The new army formations really cleaned up."

They talked for a few minutes, and then Magsaysay drew him aside. "When you are finished, stop by my office. There's something I'd like to discuss with you."

"I'll be there."

A little over an hour later, Loren sat in front of Magsaysay's desk. The lean Filipino sat back in his chair. "Thank you for coming. I always seem to function better in official surroundings. I'll come right to the point. The Philippine Government would like you to be head of our covert operations organization here in the Islands. We desperately need a structured, intelligence gathering mechanism and a research and analysis function to process intelligence data. We would like to see it modeled after your CIA. It is a very important post, and we need your considerable talents to make it work."

"You mean to leave the United States and live here for however long it would take?"

"We hope that you would consider making the Philippine Islands your home. We have come to think of you as one of us, because we have been through so much together."

Loren was stunned. Finally, he found his voice. "I'm pleased that your government has the confidence in me to offer me such a challenging task. The whole idea of building such an organization is fascinating."

"Will you consider this offer?"

"Yes, of course!" Loren paused. "I have to tell you that the idea of leaving my own country, my career with the CIA, and my professional and personal associations would be a difficult decision for me. I need some time to consider."

"I understand. I'm sure you have many questions on the practical implementation of such a step. If you want to discuss these issues, I will make sure that the appropriate people are available to answer your questions."

"Thank you, Ramon. I am honored."

Magsaysay rose to shake his hand. "You have ties here now, Loren. Remember them as well when you decide."

He thought of Maria. "Yes, Ramon, I will."

Dinner at the Castillejos' was a jubilant affair. Everyone was in animated conversation about the spectacular military campaign against the Huks. When asked how he felt about the campaign, Loren praised the Filipino fighting man. "It's really their victory. Without them, it never could have happened." No one at the house that night knew of his role in the operation.

Maria had greeted him at the door, but they really hadn't had a chance to talk. "Come walk with me on the terrace, Loren." A full moon shone on them in the beautiful late summer night. They strolled with her arm through his. "There has been talk that there were people up in the mountains spotting the Huk positions."

"Really?"

"It was you up there, wasn't it?"

"You know I can't talk about things like that, Maria."

"Yes, I know, but it was, wasn't it?" Loren was silent.

"All right, you don't have to tell me, but I know." They strolled further down the wide terrace. "Loren, my father says that

Magsaysay wants you to remain here with us in the Philippines. He wants you to be head of an important government organization."

"He talked with me this afternoon. I didn't know what to say. A decision to take on something like that is so large that I told him I needed time to consider it."

Maria stopped in front of him and reached out to touch his hands. She looked into his eyes. "Stay here with me, Loren. We love each other! I will bear you fine, strong sons!"

She was in his arms and he held her closely. "I know, my love, I know."

The next few days saw momentous events in the Islands. Summary arrests were made of members of the Politburo, the organ of Communist leadership in the Philippines. All the records of the Communist Party were confiscated. In conjunction with this, the government suspended the right of habeas corpus for suspected Huks. A rumor was circulating that Ramon Magsaysay was out in the field with his troops, sharing their rations and bivouacking with them. Loren, heartened by the news, relaxed from the campaign in the mountains.

When the final figures became available, Loren saw that the government forces killed or captured a large number of Huks and their leaders during Operation Hammer. Now the army was following up with an effort to disrupt Huk communications, to eliminate their sources of information, and to destroy their supplies. Ultimately, their aim was to destroy the rest of the enemy leadership.

The government issued press releases praising the Huks who had seen the error of their ways and had informed government sources of the whereabouts of Huk concentrations and leadership. In this, Loren saw the hand of Lansdale, the psychological warfare expert. He was happy to see the way that the Government, in the person of Magsaysay, was following up on their successful operation.

They were also dealing with street violence in Manila, which had become so common that Loren's altercation with the street gang had gone unreported. The inquiries that Manuel Castillejos made turned up nothing. Loren would never know what happened to the combatants. The Government was now taking strong measures to gain control of the streets. The future looked bright, he thought.

CHAPTER XXVII—THE DISCOVERY

Loren struggled with the weighty decisions he knew he would have to make. He felt the need to get completely away from everything for a few days to think. He had another thing that he felt he had to undertake as well, a sort of pilgrimage. Washington approved Loren's request for an extension of his stay in the Philippines by cable the previous day. He was officially on leave for a month.

He talked to Maria about it. "I've got to get away. I've got to think all of this through."

"I want to come with you, Loren. We can find a quiet beach somewhere and lie in the sand, and talk about these things."

"This is something that I have to do by myself, Maria."

She was downcast. "Where will you go?"

"I'm thinking that I'll go back to Mindanao. That's where it all began."

She looked at him with her soft brown eyes. "I'll be here for you, Loren." Then she was in his arms.

The following morning he took a cab down to the Manila docks and bought a ticket on the interisland steamer to Cagayen on the island of Mindanao. As it was a two-day trip, he decided to get an outside cabin for the voyage.

As the old steamer chugged its way down the sea lanes to the south, Loren reflected on the last time he had run down this series of inland seas. They did not follow the exact route he took in 1942, but parts of it he remembered very clearly. Toward the end of the second day, they sighted Cagayen and, an hour later, were at the dock. Loren found a hotel and then set about trying to find a jeep for hire. At the second garage he tried he was successful and arranged to pick it up the next day.

As he walked through the hotel lobby, a young Filipino came up to him. "Excuse me sir, my name is Porfirio Diaz and I'm a reporter for the *Cagayen Banner*. Do I understand correctly that you are Commander Middleton, the guerrilla leader?"

"Yes, I'm Middleton. What can I do for you?"

"Sir, will you grant me the privilege of an interview? Many of the people here remember you and your fight against the Japanese."

"Sure. Let's sit here in the lobby and you can fire away." A half-hour later, the young reporter thanked him profusely and left for his office at the newspaper. After dinner, Loren walked around the downtown area of Cagayen to get a feel for life in the real Philippines again, away from the glitter of Manila.

Early the following morning, he picked up his jeep and set out on a road, leading northeast toward Surigao. The paved road ran along the coast, with dirt roads leading to the interior. Then the pavement ended and he found himself bumping along a dirt track toward the fishing village from which he had left Mindanao in a great hurry seven years before.

Loren parked the jeep on the village's main street and set about trying to find the village headman. In a half-hour, he was successful. The man was surprised that Loren could converse in Visayan and had a great deal to say about many things. Finally, Loren asked him about Ramon.

"Ramon Vargas? Oh, he is a legend around here, a great hero. He fought the Japanese. He and the American, Middleton. There was a big battle up in the hills. They killed many. No one has seen him since those days. Did you know him?"

"Yes, I did."

Disappointed, Loren returned to his jeep and motored beyond the village. In a few minutes he saw it, the rocky inlet they had used to land on Mindanao. He stood looking over the water as the memories flooded over him. He knew that somewhere out toward the middle of the sound, in the deep part, was the 25 boat, the craft that had brought them here from Bataan in those dark, terrible days.

He returned to the jeep and doubled back toward the town. In a short while, he found the narrow, dusty road that led up into the mountains. Loren cranked the jeep into a lower gear and proceeded to climb away from the shore. The road twisted and turned as he climbed higher. Then, there was a relatively straight part and he arrived at Ramon's village.

He knew that the village was deserted, but what greeted him was a shock. Burned to the ground, it was completely devoid of any trace of life. He got out and walked through the charred remains. Part of the jungle trail that led down to the sea was still visible. The trail leading to the south along the mountains was completely overgrown. He paused for a minute where Ramon's house had been. Nothing was there now to suggest that people had lived there at one time. While looking for the trail to the stream, he came upon a graveyard. A score of graves were marked with crosses, but no names. He wondered who they might be and whether perhaps there was someone he knew, buried in that lonely place.

As he strode back to the jeep, he looked down the road and remembered the last time he had seen Tomi. If she were still alive, she would be out there somewhere in one of the hundreds of villages in the mountains or the verdant forest, some of them not even on a map. Or perhaps she would have gone to Cagayen or one of the other larger towns. He hoped that, wherever she and their child were, they were healthy and well. He started the jeep and drove back down the dusty dirt road.

Late in the afternoon, Loren returned to the hotel. He planned to return to Manila on the interisland steamer the next morning and then take an overnight flight on Pan American to the U.S. The sunlight was quite bright and he had a problem seeing when he entered the hotel lobby. As he strode to the desk for his key, he perceived a woman and a young child standing, watching him. As his vision became accustomed to the gloom, he suddenly saw who it was. He hurried toward them.

He held her closely. She was crying. "My God, Tomi, I've been searching for you since the end of the war! Even the Philippine Government couldn't find you!" Then he saw the young girl watching them. She was quite tall for a Filipino child and very pretty, with pale white skin. "Tomi?"

"Yes, Loren, she is our daughter. Juanita, this is the man I have told you about. This is your father." The child looked at him with large, somber eyes and said nothing. "I have many things to tell you. Is there someplace we can go?"

"Of course. We'll go to my room. Have you eaten yet?"

"No."

"I'll have something sent up when we get there."

They spent the next two hours over dinner reliving what had happened to them since Tomi had left the village. Loren watched her as they spoke. Tomi was fuller bodied than the young girl she had been eight years ago, but she was as pretty as ever. He couldn't help but remember her in those first full days when they were together and in love.

Overcome with emotion, they relived the incredible, tumultuous times. The young girl listened intently to all of this as they ate, saying very little other than an occasional polite thank you.

"What of Ramon, Tomi?"

"No one has seen or heard of my father since the Japanese came to the village that day. Our people are scattered all over Northern Mindanao, so information is hard to come by. I think he must have been killed by the Japanese."

"I'm sorry." He turned to the little girl. "And what about Nita?"

"She was born on July 8, 1943. She is seven now. She is a very bright child."

They talked a while longer and then Tomi excused herself for a moment to go to the bathroom. The two of them, Loren and his daughter, were alone together. The girl looked at him. "Are you really my father?" Her question was like a voice from the past, the precise, unaccented English.

Loren took in the unmistakable heredity of the girl. "Yes, Nita, I am."

Tomi returned to the room and sat on the edge of the bed, her hands crossed in her lap. "There are other things we must discuss, Loren. I am married now. My husband and I have two children of our own. It is not easy here in the Philippines these days. I came here tonight hoping that you might be able to help Juanita a little. Her prospects are not very good as it stands."

"I would like to meet your husband, Tomi, and we can discuss it. There are several things we could do to help her. By the way, I am married too. Do you remember Beverly?"

"Of course. You two are married, truly? I would have thought the other one, the one who had strong feelings for you."

"JoAnne was captured by the Japanese when the village was overrun. It has not been easy for her, but she is home in the U.S. now."

"Do you have children?"

"No. Bev had a difficult miscarriage and she can't have children now."

"I am sorry, Loren. We must go now. I will write down our address for you. You will come to lunch?"

"Yes. Oh, how did you know I was here?" She wordlessly showed him the large front-page story about his visit in the *Cagayen Banner.*

After they had gone, he sat for a long while, thinking. He was overwhelmed by the events of the day. He knew that he must make sure that his daughter was cared for. The other decisions he came here to make weighed even more heavily, now. Somehow, there had to be a way.

The next few days were days of discovery for all of them. Tomi's husband met him at the door when he arrived the next day and welcomed him to his house. He was a recently graduated lawyer and was struggling to establish a practice. Nita, after her initial reticence, warmed to him and was constantly at his side. The other children stared at him in wonder. Loren had a hard time getting used to the idea of being a famous person there on Mindanao.

Loren sent a series of cables to both the United States and Philippine Governments to determine his legal status regarding his daughter. In the intervening time, while he waited for a reply, Loren spent as much time as he could with Nita. She was a warm, outgoing child and they talked easily. The day when Nita joined him for lunch at the hotel was a memorable event. Loren called for her in a cab at her home. Moments later, he entered the dining room with Nita, dressed in her Sunday best, on his arm.

Loren told her about where he and Bev lived in Chevy Chase and what it was like. "Have you seen pictures of the United States capital building?"

"The big white building with the dome? Oh, yes!"

"Well, it is about thirty minutes from our house. That and the White House, where the American President lives." He went on to tell her about the city and its many attractions. She seemed to hang on every word. The two of them did something every day as they waited. The experience was unique for both of them.

They had still heard nothing, so Loren decided that he needed to go to Manila and the US Embassy to expedite the process. He called Tomi to apprise her of his decision.

"When will you return, Loren?

"As soon as I get news regarding my application for Nita's citizenship. I have a month of leave to sort this out."

"She's going to miss you, Loren. Please, hurry back."

Later, he talked with Nita. "You are going away, Father?"

"For a little while, yes."

"Will you come back?"

"Of course I will, Nita."

After he had checked into the Manila Hotel, he caught a cab to the southern suburbs and Maria. He wasn't looking forward to telling her what had happened. They walked on the terrace again as they spoke. "Maria, we haven't talked much about the war."

"No, we haven't."

"When I was up in the mountains of Mindanao, when the Japs were hunting us, there was a girl. We had a child."

She stopped short and looked at him levelly, her eyes not wavering. "You had a child…with a Filipino girl?"

"Yes. The reason that I'm telling you now is that when I was in Cagayen, she came to me…with the child."

Maria continued to look at him, saying nothing. Loren saw that there were tears in her eyes. "So what do you want to do, Loren, marry her?"

"She is already married, to a young lawyer who is just starting out. She has two children by him."

"I see. Does your wife know about this?"

"She was there in the mountains with us, she and another nurse. I haven't told her yet about finding Nita."

"Is that the child's name, Nita?"

"Juanita."

"I think you had better tell your wife."

"Yes."

"What do you want to do, then, Loren?"

"It is not easy for them now, financially. I want to help her and I want to see that she becomes a United States citizen."

"You can't do this, Loren. It will damage your personal position here, limit how far you can go in government service. Pay the girl money if you must but don't acknowledge her. I have grown up in these circles. I know how they work."

"I can't do that, Maria. I have seen her. We have done things together. I can't."

"You must think about this. Promise me you will think about it before making a final decision."

"Yes…by all means."

At mid morning the next day, the phone rang in Loren's room at the Manila Hotel. Manuel Castillejos was on the other end. "Good morning, Loren. I was wondering if we could meet for lunch today."

"Certainly. Where would you like to have lunch?"

"There's no better restaurant than at your hotel. Can we meet at, say, twelve thirty?"

"I'll get us a reservation. See you then."

Manuel Castillejos was sipping a cocktail as they waited for their main course. Manuel seemed to Loren to be just a bit cool toward him as they spoke. "Maria has told us about you and her. Also, about the child on Mindanao. What she has told you about the mores of our society is true. If you acknowledge the child, born out of wedlock, the Catholic Church would condemn you for it. That is very important here. It will cause you trouble, working for the Philippine government."

"I understand what you are telling me, Manuel, but I can't turn my back on her. I am in the process of making application for US citizenship for her."

"What about Maria, Loren? She tells me that you and she are in love and have been for a long time."

"We shouldn't have to destroy my daughter's life to make things good for us. I just can't accept that. My God, Manuel, this all happened a long time ago. It was wartime. Surely you haven't forgotten how things were?"

"No, my friend. No, I haven't. Unfortunately, it is not I who will pass judgement on you." They had a quiet lunch, with neither of them having much to say. Then Manuel laid aside his napkin. "I have an appointment so I must leave you. Maria says that you promised to think about this before making a decision. I implore you, please take the time to do so. Goodbye for now."

At the US Embassy, Loren received confirmation that, with the proper paperwork, Nita would legally become his daughter and subsequently a citizen of the United States of America. Because she had been born in the Philippines, she was eligible for dual citizenship.

Back at the hotel, Loren decided that it was time for Bev to know. With some difficulty, he was finally able to place a call to her. When she answered, her voice seemed very far away. "Bev, I have something to tell you. I have found Tomi and the child."

"Oh, Loren!" Even over the noisy telephone line, he could hear the emotion in her voice.

"Tomi is married now and has two children by her husband. They are struggling somewhat, because economic conditions here are not very good. Tomi found me by accident and approached me to see if I could help with Nita. That is her name, Juanita."

"What do you want to do?"

"We are looking at what might be done now."

Bev was quiet for a moment before she spoke. "Loren, bring her back with you."

"Is that what you want me to do?"

"Yes."

"Tomi and her husband would have to agree. Nita would have to want it too. Are you sure, Bev?"

Bev was silent for another moment. "Oh, yes, Loren. If they agree, I would love to have her here with us." He heard a warmth in her voice that had not been there for a long time.

Loren filed the necessary applications through the U.S. Embassy and more time passed. Then he received word that Immigration and Naturalization had approved Nita's petition. She was officially an American! Loren made initial inquiries regarding travel arrangements to the U.S.

As the time approached for him to leave for the States, he returned to Cagayen and met again with Tomi and her husband. He spoke to them, earnestly. "I have thought a lot about Juanita and what would be the best for her. If she would like to go, I propose that she come back to the States with me and live in Washington. I've talked to Bev and she wants Nita to live with us too. We can come back to the Philippines in the summer and you would all be welcome to visit us at any time."

Tomi was concerned. "That would be a big change for Juanita. She wouldn't know anyone. Do you think she would be accepted by the American children?"

"Social attitudes in the U.S. have changed tremendously since the war. I believe from what I have seen that Nita would have no problems. A lot of children from foreign lands have come to the U.S. because of the war. She would be one of many." They left it that Tomi and her husband would discuss what he had proposed.

A week before his planned departure, Tomi came to him. "Loren, I have talked with my husband and we have agreed to your proposal, if Juanita wants to go. I would miss her so very much, but if we could see her like you said, I think it would be a wonderful thing."

"We will see what she says."

That night, in their living room, Tomi asked the girl about it. "Your father would like you to go to the United States and live with him. Would you like to do this?"

"But Mommy, I would miss you so much!"

"He has promised to bring you home to me in the summers so that we can be together. We will see each other often. It is a great opportunity for you to live in America. Your father can do so many things for you there."

Nita was quiet for a moment, and then she looked at Loren. Her gaze was steady. "Yes, I would like to go to live in America with Father."

Maria and Loren were alone in the house in the suburbs as they talked. She was quiet and withdrawn as he spoke. "I'm returning to the states with Nita tomorrow. I'm sorry, Maria. I couldn't just discard her. It has nothing to do with her mother. That was all so long ago."

"My father says that you have rejected Magsaysay's offer."

"Yes. For a number of reasons, I felt that I needed to stay in Washington."

"What now, Loren?"

"I'll be returning to the Philippines in a few months, as usual. We need to use this time to consider all that has happened."

"Yes, Loren. Yes, we do."

Loren cabled Bev that they were coming. The next day, Bev replied that she would be waiting for them. Someone, at last, would use the children's furniture in the upstairs bedroom that had been unused for so long.

CHAPTER XXVIII—DENOUEMENT

They had a beautiful spring day for it. The sun was shining brilliantly and there was just the hint of a breeze. Beverly was putting the final touches on the picnic hamper with Nita helping her. Loren had just finished loading towels, swimsuits, blankets, suntan lotion and the badminton equipment in the trunk of their new Mercury. He watched the two of them as they put plastic containers and foil wrapped items into the large basket. All the maternal feelings that Bev had kept within herself for so long had spilled out in great abundance since the little girl had come. The two of them had become very close and they were always together.

When he made the decision to bring Nita home to the house in Chevy Chase, he hadn't realized that it would be for Beverly as much as it was for him. A month or so after Nita arrived, Loren and Bev talked out on the porch late at night.

"I would never have believed that having Nita here would work out so well. Are you really happy, Bev?"

"It's a new beginning for me, Loren."

"You were so much against adoption."

"This isn't like adoption. We can never have children who are part of you and me. She is part of you, Loren, and I love her for it. I feel like I'm whole again. I've never been so happy."

"We're a family again."

"Yes, that's the way it should be."

The previous Monday, he had been to a meeting at the Philippine Embassy. Jorge Gonzales, one of the Embassy officials came up to him afterwards. "Loren, I wanted to take this opportunity to say goodbye. I've been ordered back to Manila."

"Bigger and better things, Jorge?"

"I hope so. By the way, I think you know my replacement, Manuel Castillejos."

Loren was stunned. "Manuel, coming here?"

"Yes, he and his family will be arriving in a few days. He asked me especially to say hello and tell you that he would be seeing you soon."

"Thank you, Jorge. If you talk to him, tell him I'm looking forward to seeing him again."

Back in his office, Loren was deep in thought. Maria here in Washington, minutes away! Despite their recent differences, he knew that he would only have to pick up the phone and she would be in his arms. He knew deep down that he had to resolve this part of his life, at last.

The following week, he received a letter from Maria. Her words were full of excitement as she told him about her father's assignment to the Philippine Embassy and about their imminent arrival in Washington. She would be here before he knew it.

The Central Intelligence Agency was referred to as "The Company" by those who worked there, so it was with a great deal of jocularity that Loren's fellow employees talked about the "Company" Picnic that had been organized for this Saturday. A park bordering on the Potomac was the site for it, and the Middletons were just about ready to head out. A half-hour later they pulled into the parking lot at the picnic site. Loren found a table that had a bit of shade and they comfortably spread out for the afternoon.

"Daddy, can we go swimming now?" Nita asked.

"Let's have our lunch first, and then the three of us can go take a dip later."

Beverly, elegant even in her white shorts and blue top was glowing. Loren was wearing his swim trunks and a faded Washington Redskins T-shirt. He had brought his canvas tennis shoes in anticipation of some badminton later in the afternoon. He was in the midst of getting their lunch from the picnic basket when he saw a man and a woman moving toward their table. With a start, he realized that it was Manuel Castillejos and Maria! He had no idea they would be here so soon! He fought to control his emotions.

"My God, where have you two dropped from?" he stammered. "Hello Manuel, hello Maria!" Loren moved forward to shake hands. With an enormous effort, he managed to control his outward reactions. Maria's hand lingered in his for a moment. She was wearing fashionable brown toreador trousers and a white blouse that showed her off to great advantage.

"Manuel, you remember my wife Beverly. And this is Manuel's daughter, Maria."

Manuel moved forward and took Bev's hand. "So pleased to see you again, Senora Middleton."

"I'm Bev," she said, with a radiant smile. Welcome to America. You too, Maria."

"I am pleased to meet you."

At that moment, Nita ran up to them. She stopped when she saw the others.

Loren took her hand. "And this is my daughter Nita."

Maria looked at the beautiful young girl. "Hello, Nita."

"I am very pleased to meet you," Nita replied in her flawless English.

Maria looked at Loren. "We had heard of your good fortune in finding her." She took Nita by the hands. "Oh, Loren, she is precious!"

"Thank you, Maria." He tried to keep his voice at an even timbre. "We were very fortunate in finding one another." They went on to talk about Manuel's appointment to the Embassy, and all the adjustments that they would have to make.

Bev listened and commiserated. "If I can be of any help, please call me."

"Thank you. We have to go look at a house now. Aileen, my wife, is waiting for us. We just stopped by for a few minutes."

"We're glad you did. We'll have to get together once you are settled." Maria was watching him as he spoke. They said their goodbyes and the Castillejos walked away toward the parking lot. Loren fought the urge to exhale sharply.

Nita went off to play with some of the other children and Loren finished distributing the contents of the picnic hamper.

Bev looked at him. "She is lovely and she likes you, Loren."

Loren measured his reply. "Yes, she is lovely. When I first met her, she was quite young. A long time ago, just after the end of the war."

A reception for the new officials would take place at the Philippine Embassy the following Friday evening. Loren and Bev had received a beautifully engraved invitation. Bev had scheduled a hair appointment at her salon on Thursday afternoon. As she was about to leave, a call from the school informed her that Nita had taken ill and needed to come home.

That evening, she discussed the situation with Loren. "Why don't you go ahead without me this time, Loren. Nita is running a temperature, and I don't expect her to be a whole lot better by tomorrow night."

"I was looking forward to us attending this gala. It may be the best do of the year. I'm sorry you're going to miss it."

"I know that a lot of important things get decided at these functions." She looked at him in a way that he wondered about. "Why don't you do what you have to do and come home early? I'll wait up."

"I'll do that."

The reception was indeed a glittering affair. Seas of well-dressed people were everywhere and the ball gowns were truly marvelous. After a few minutes, he saw Maria in the crowd and went to her.

She turned to him with a beautiful smile. "Beverly is not with you tonight?"

"No. Nita is ill." He looked into her eyes. "We need to talk, Maria. Is there somewhere we can go?"

"There's always the terrace." Memories of other times came to him as they walked together in the summer night. Maria put her arm through his. "I'm so glad that we're here now, here where we can be together."

"What about Nita, Maria?"

"Here in the United States, it is different."

"How is that?"

"Here in the U.S. we don't have to be concerned with island society or the Church because of her."

"You'll have to go back home one day."

"I want to be here with you. We love each other. Nothing has changed."

"Yes, it has, Maria. We have to consider Nita now. I will personally see to it that she is not a problem for anyone."

Maria paused for a moment and then turned to him, placing her hands on his arm. She spoke, wistfully. "I've lost you, haven't I? To a beautiful eight-year-old child."

Emotions flooded over him. "This is the way it has to be, Maria." His voice sounded strange and unnatural to him.

Maria looked away. "We would have had beautiful children too, but maybe that's for another life."

He watched her, so lovely in the moonlight. "I will never forget you, Maria."

"Nor I you." Tears shone in her eyes. "Go with God, Loren." She turned from him and walked away. As he watched her go, Loren had an overwhelming sense of loss.

A month later, Loren invited Manuel Castillejos and his wife Aileen for a round of golf at the CIA's country club. As they were walking down the fairway, Loren asked about Maria. "Oh, she has decided to pursue her graduate studies at the University of California. She has an apartment in Berkeley and is thoroughly enjoying going to school there. Their International Studies Department is one of the best."

"That's what I understand. Please give her my best."

CHAPTER XXIX—EPILOGUE

The war against the Huks went on for another two years and there were small, hard-core bands that carried on beyond that, but from the summer of Operation Hammer, they were plainly in eclipse. Thoroughly shaken and driven to excesses, the Huks committed acts that destroyed their popular base. Government forces killed or captured many of their best leaders. Their top man, Turac, continued to elude the government forces diligently searching for him. Then, with dissension and disagreements within their ranks, Turac surrendered to the authorities, two years after Hammer.

In pursuit of his goals Magsaysay, the pragmatist, would convert captured Huks to his side and use them against their former comrades. The intensification of military intelligence activities and psychological warfare efforts against the Huks was under the guidance of Magsaysay's American advisor, Colonel Lansdale. On his advice, the Philippine Government undertook pacification of the Huks by offering land or jobs if they would defect. The strategy was ultimately a winning one.

After the defeat of the Huks, the crest of the wave receded from the Philippines and it became pretty much a backwater in the Asian scene. Korea and then Southeast Asia became the focal points in the fight to contain communism. Loren became more involved in these theaters of operation and spent less time on Philippine matters.

His official visits to the Islands were few and usually in conjunction with some other efforts in Southeast Asia.

Loren was happy to see his friend Carlos Romulo become the Ambassador to Washington in 1952. Then, in a tumultuous election, Ramon Magsaysay became President in late 1953, defeating the incumbent Quirino. He died in an airplane crash a few years later, a tragic time for his country. The Philippine Islands nation carried on through all of this with little change in their day-to-day life...now that the enemy was no more.

The start of Commencement exercises at the high school in Chevy Chase was only a short time away. Nita, draped over an easy chair in the living room, was having an extended telephone conversation with her best friend, Beth. Loren watched his daughter bubble over with laughter as she talked. Today she would address the assembled parents and students as Valedictorian of her class. Nita was a beauty of the first order...tall, pale and willowy, with long, dark brown hair. The oriental cast of her eyes reflected her Maylayan heritage and gave her an exotic touch. She spoke exceptionally well, as she would demonstrate again at Commencement.

"You had better start thinking of getting ready, Nita. It's less than two hours now."

"OK, Dad." She signed off with Beth and bounded upstairs to her room. She would go to Georgetown University in the fall, with a major in International Studies. Nita's steady boyfriend, Jim Storey, was completing his second year there. They had met in high school and had been together pretty much ever since. She was looking forward with great anticipation to being an undergraduate in the fall.

Her trips to the Far East with her father as she was growing up had developed her interest in Asian languages and culture. She was fluent in French, Tagalog, Visayan and a collection of Southeast Asian dialects. The time she had spent with her mother in the summers only whetted her appetite for learning about Asia.

Tomi and her husband Luis were now living in Manila where he was working in the Government's legal division. Loren's sponsorship was instrumental in bringing this about.

The summer before last, the Middletons had gone to Manila for their annual trip, now that Tomi and Luis were there. Loren and Bev went back to Corregidor for the first time since the terrible days of 1941-42. Nita had come with them, along with Tomi and the younger children.

Walking toward the entrance to Malinta Tunnel, Loren told them about when he had been there all those years ago. "When we weren't out fighting the Japanese, we sometimes were tasked with delivering military dispatches from Bataan to the headquarters in the tunnel. The seat of government of the Philippines was there, as well as the military headquarters during that time."

"Were they shooting at you?" asked Nita.

"A good part of the time we were getting shelled or bombed when we were here on the island."

Bev stood for a moment at the tunnel entrance. "I worked as a nurse in the tunnel, in the underground hospital lateral. It seems so long ago now."

Nita shook her head. "It all sounds really scary."

"I was scared all the time," answered Loren.

Bev took Loren's arm. "So was I."

"I don't believe it. Not you two. Not after all you've been through."

"It's the truth, Nita."

The younger generation had varying levels of interest in what they saw, but as the two families passed by the stark ruins with the great guns still pointing skyward, Loren had the feeling that they were not alone. This was especially true when they walked through the tunnel, where so many things had happened.

He talked to Bev about it afterwards at their hotel. "Did you feel the ghosts out there in the ruins like I did, Bev?"

A look of surprise came over her face. "Yes, Loren. Yes, I did. I thought it was just me." They didn't speak of it again.

Recently, Tomi and Luis visited the Middletons as part of a reunion that Beverly had initiated and planned. The experience was a remarkable one for them all, having the survivors of their time in the Philippines together under one roof again. At a nearby motel where the out-of-town people had gathered, they had a formal dinner where they remembered those incredible times.

Loren gave a short speech of welcome. "It's wonderful that we are all together once again. We've got a lot of catching up to do for the last few years. Before we start, I'd like to offer a toast." He raised his glass. "To our fallen comrades." The room was quiet as they drank.

During the course of the evening, Loren and Bev talked with all of the attendees. They had maintained close ties with the Buchmans who lived closeby, but they had not seen some of the others since they left the Philippines. Ed Thomas, their unofficial quartermaster, had retired from the navy and was now teaching school in Poughkeepsie, New York. Jess Roe, who had resurrected the 25 boat, had left the navy after the war and now had his own filling station in Great Falls, Montana. Rod Wells had taken advantage of his visibility as a well-known returning veteran to get into radio, and later television. He managed a local TV station in Cincinnati, Ohio. Mike Hanson, another navy retiree, had a hardware store in Minneapolis, Minnesota.

Tom Kite and his wife Felice had made the long trip from Manila as well. She was as pretty as Loren remembered her. He was glad to see Tom again after all the experiences they had shared in their lives.

Loren and Bev were in deep conversation with Tom and Felice when, out of the corner of his eye, Loren saw another couple enter the room. He turned to look. On the arm of a middle-aged, graying man was JoAnne!

"Bev…"

"Yes, Loren?" and then she saw them too. Loren was on his feet and moving toward the couple. After a moment, Bev rose and followed.

JoAnne looked up as he came toward her. "Loren!" Then they were embracing.

"JoAnne, it's so good to see you!" He held both her hands.

"It's good to see you as well! Loren, this is my husband, Jim Hall." The two men shook hands.

Loren turned to the rest. "Look who is here!" The others crowded around JoAnne and her husband. Everyone was talking a mile a minute. Loren watched her as she responded. After all these years, she was still pretty, but the lines in her face said much.

Finally, he intervened. "Jim, JoAnne, come sit over here. It going to take us awhile to get caught up." They talked for a long time.

Today, the sun was shining brilliantly and there was just the slightest trace of a breeze. They would have a good day for Commencement, Loren decided. Nita was still upstairs getting ready when Bev returned from shopping. As she came into the house, she called out to Loren. "I think I have everything in house for the reception afterward. Can you think of anything we've overlooked?" She had grayed somewhat, as had Loren, but her hairdresser neatly disguised it. She was as slender and elegant as the day that they were married.

He smiled at her. "I think we are ready."

Loren and his boss Pat McFadden had prospered since the days in the Philippines. Loren now had the responsibility for Southeast Asia operations, while Pat headed up the Far East organization. Loren was looking forward to the CIA's imminent move to their spacious new headquarters in Langley, Virginia. Loren and Beverly were considering a move of their own to a country estate in the rural Virginia countryside, a large spacious home with extensive grounds. His commute would be much shorter, but Bev was having a problem giving up the house in Chevy Chase that she had spent so much time on.

Since Dien Bien Phu, the two Vietnams and their Asian neighbors were the center of attention for the CIA. U.S. military advisors were in the field with the South Vietnamese troops now and the path forward was not at all clear. Washington had proposed many operations for the area and decisions were forthcoming. Loren had never gone to the field again after those last heady days in the Philippines against the Huks. His experienced direction of projects in that part of the world had drawn much praise and many honors had come his way.

The time to leave had arrived and Loren pointed their new Continental toward the high school. Twenty minutes later, they pulled into the parking lot. They found seats close to the podium and Nita left them to get ready. He wished that Tomi and Luis could have been here on this special day, but government business had kept Luis in Manila.

Loren glanced around him and saw several familiar faces. Jim Storey and his family were two rows behind them and they exchanged greetings. Pat and Ellen McFadden were there, as were Bob and Cara Lee. Their nine-year-old son was quite a handful, according to Bob. He waved to both couples. They would all be joining Loren and Bev at their home for the reception afterward.

A half-hour later, Nita stood at the podium in her cap and gown for her address. Her eyes were shining as she began. "I would like to start by thanking my parents and this big, wonderful country..."

ABOUT THE AUTHOR

Before his early retirement from U.S. Government service, Mr. Littleton spent many years working in the intelligence community and the Department of Defense. His military experience was with the Marine Corps where he spent time in Japan and Korea. He has lived in Australia, South Africa, and the U.K., and has traveled extensively in Europe, and Africa. He researched "Guerrilla!" in the Philippines.

Mr. Littleton has previously published "The Knights of Malta," about World War II, and "The Cajun," a story of Southeast Asia. He bases much of what he writes on personal experiences. He holds a Bachelor of Science degree in Mathematics from Lewis and Clark College in Portland, Oregon. He lives in Ridgecrest, California with his wife and two daughters.